23 WOODCOCK IN 22 YEARS

23 WOODCOCK IN 22 YEARS

Reflections on Hunting, the Night Sky,

and Our Place in the Universe

JEFF WILKERSON

University of Iowa Press, Iowa City

University of Iowa Press, Iowa City 52242
Copyright © 2024 by Jeff Wilkerson
uipress.uiowa.edu
Printed in the United States of America

ISBN: 978-1-60938-987-1 (pbk)
ISBN: 978-1-60938-988-8 (ebk)

Design by Ashley Muehlbauer

Printed on acid-free paper

Catalog-in-Publication data is on file at the Library of Congress.

Illustrations by L'Engle Charis-Carlson

The quotation from Purcell's Nobel lecture appears in E. M. Purcell—Nobel Lecture, NobelPrize.org, Nobel Prize Outreach AB 2023, Monday, October 9, 2023, https://www.nobelprize.org/prizes/physics/1952/purcell/lecture/.

In memory of my mother

CONTENTS

YEAR 1

A Homecoming

The story stretching before us is, in part, one of how hunting woodcock, a bird I knew almost nothing about for most of the span of my existence, became an integral part of my life, anchoring me to both a new place and my own history, providing me one avenue into feeling the flow of time and sensing the network of connections that bind us one to another through time and space. In addition to being a woodcock hunter, I am, among many other things, an astronomer. Astronomy serves as a distinct avenue into those same feelings of temporal and spatial connections, sometimes running parallel to the woodcock hunting avenue, sometimes intersecting it. The result is a resonance between hunting a russet migratory bird about the size of a robin and, as Lee Ann Womack urged in her song "I Hope You Dance," giving the heavenly vault its due.

Often people do not recognize astronomy as the application of the laws of physics to our universe at large and the structures within the universe. My degrees are all from physics departments, and in my world, there is no meaningful demarcation between astronomy and physics. In the past, I could use this to my advantage when settling into airplane seats. When world-weary and in no mood to chat, in response to my neighbor asking, "What do you do?" I'd respond, "I am a physicist," usually shutting down further chit-chat. If I answered, "I'm an astronomer," people were delighted to chat, even if occasionally they were seeking to have a horoscope cast. It's possible that approach wouldn't work anymore, if the popular television show *The Big Bang Theory* has made physics so glamorous that everyone wants to talk about it incessantly.

My approach to airplane socializing failed me utterly one time, when I was flying from my native Indiana to my then current California home following my grandfather's funeral. The poor pastor who served as officiant at the funeral had never met my grandfather. He circulated before the service to gather stories from the family, leading me to recall the times we chased schools of white bass tearing through shad on the surface of The Lake, harvesting vegetables from the garden designed to feed the entire extended family throughout the year, and cracking nuts at the picnic table under the hickory tree, where my grandmother was certain that ticks were falling onto my head and disappearing into my suspiciously long hair in droves. Although not aware enough to recognize it at the time, it was then that my need to be back closer to the land, away from the urban sprawl, began to grow inside me, even though I had been in graduate school only a year.

On the flight from Chicago to Oakland, I absentmindedly worked physics problems, mostly to pass the time but also in preparation for the upcoming qualifying exam, a delightful event that consisted of a six-hour written exam covering classical physics one Saturday, a six-hour written exam covering modern physics the next Saturday, and two one-hour oral exams on these topics a week later. As I worked away, my neighbor in the next seat leaned over and said, "I hope you don't plan to do Lagrangian mechanics all the way back to California." Busted by a former physics professor. It took another nine years from that point to my sitting on the back porch of my house in Iowa, watching the hazy glow of the Milky Way appear above me. With me never in a hurry to force things, it was more than another three years from that first Iowa night under the stars until I became a woodcock hunter.

When I arrived in northeast Iowa, my home now for twenty-five years, one piece of property quickly became my special go-to place. It is a large tract of public land, very large by local standards—stretching into the thousands of acres—with heavily wooded limestone bluffs that border a beautiful, clear trout stream, following the stream's path to a river that in turn tumbles to the Mississippi. The forest was open along the creek bottom, but pockets were dense on the bluffs. The bluff tops contained large stretches of cornfields and prairie grass, a microcosm of the larger northeast Iowa landscape that served as a perfect place for me to dig in and learn this new country. I explored far and wide but spent more time at this special place than anywhere else. Twelve of my first twenty-five Iowa birds were bagged here, both the reason for and result of my dedicating so much time to the property. The first wood duck I bagged along the creek remains the only banded duck I have ever taken.

One of the more interesting locations within this larger piece of land is a spot I refer to as "the old homestead," a clearing of a few acres perched near the edge of the steepest of bluffs, a sheer drop of hundreds of feet to the creek bottom below. Within the clearing are a few clumps of trees and plants of species not found anywhere else on the property and several fragments of exposed foundations of long-lost buildings. There is the smallest hint of fence melting back into the landscape on one end and corroded fragments of farm implements are scattered about. Above the bird cleaning station in my garage sits a rusted square tin that once contained Dr. Naylor Udder Balm. I filched it one day while resting at the old homestead. I have no idea exactly when the place was abandoned or why, only that the people who left the udder balm tin are gone. Of course, they aren't the first to be gone, as people deriving a living from this land were forced off it a century earlier. Any claim I have on this special place is ephemeral and not without complication. When the leaves are down, one can, while standing precariously at bluff's edge, catch glimpses of the trout stream far below. If the time is just right, the trees in one corner yield morels. A very small stand of not young but not fully mature aspen graced one end when I first encountered the site. There could have been no better spot than what we will call Old Homestead Place to begin my journey with woodcock.

By the time my life became entangled with woodcock, I was primarily a solo hunter, but my father was there for my first woodcock encounter. It's getting to be a long time since my dad has been able to hunt and a long time since he has been able to make the trek from my native southern Indiana to Iowa. Any story that spans more than two decades, as this one does, will trace much change. Many people have heard the claim that one definition of insanity (whatever that means) is doing the same thing over and over again and expecting to get a different outcome. But, of course, the world is changing moment to moment, so expecting the exact same outcome every time is actually the thing that is out of tune with how reality works. We recognize this change when we look back at the decades that have passed, but woodcock hunters see that evolution more clearly. Just as one can never step in the same river twice, one never steps into the exact same woodcock cover twice.

I grew up hunting mostly ruffed grouse, maybe the occasional bobwhite quail, with my dad, having no idea woodcock existed. Later in my Indiana hunting life, on a return from college, I am certain I saw one fly from a distant stand of mature pines encircling a small pond on property my uncle owned, property we call Grandpa Place, but I didn't know what it was. I hadn't read any of the great writers who might have enlightened me, and if the outdoor magazines I read at the time ever mentioned woodcock, it had slipped right past me.

On the eve of the most fateful day in the first year of my woodcock odyssey, my dad and I were ringing the perimeter of the old homestead, headed for the matureish aspen stand. He was out in the open while I stayed hard against the bluff edge glimpsing the creek below. Alas, my vocabulary is inadequate to describe our reaction when the woodcock flushed just a few yards in front of me, flying twenty yards before settling back onto the very edge of the bluff. We both stopped cold without shouldering a gun. Startled or stunned doesn't quite capture it. Taken aback? Confused? Awed? The knuckleball flight was definitely not grouselike, but I believe it was the sound that really got us. It was like no gamebird sound either of us had ever heard but also unlike the sound of any songbird we knew.

By this point in my life, I was a significantly better-read bird hunter than I had been just a few years earlier, leading to my certainty that this anomalous entity was a woodcock. Just as certain was that I would be a woodcock hunter. On the reflush, I still froze when the bird twittered up, offering a fine look at it. My brain was unable to connect the dots in time for it to send the appropriate message to my hands. We could have followed again but chose to let it go.

After my parents and I shared breakfast the next morning, they embarked on the long drive home. Moments after waving them away, I was changing clothes and heading back to the old homestead to see whether that bird was still in residence or whether it had been a dream. Carefully, I retraced my steps along the bluff edge, getting to the aspens where I crisscrossed the cover before pushing out onto a narrow plateau that ended in an open arc that served as a balcony deck providing the best seats available for observing the valley below. Unable to navigate farther, I turned back through the aspens and into the homestead clearing where I passed what looked like an errant Christmas tree, likely a gift left behind by the homesteaders. Pausing to ponder my next move, I heard the bird burst from the ground between me and that pine, very close. I spun about and fired in a single motion. Mere moments later, I could not recall the scene with any vividness, just a blur. A few yards away lay my first woodcock. I will make a guess that most people who ever shoot a woodcock will have bagged their first long before the age of thirty-five. There is much to be said for the drink-it-all-in rush of youth. But firsts can be uniquely rewarding, given the perspective of experience.

In my California life, the concepts of home ownership and seeing the celestial river of the Milky Way from my home had existed beyond the span of what my imagination could hold. The woodcock, now so real in my hand, had lain even further beyond the bounds of my imagination. Much has been written about the odd anatomy of a woodcock, with the oft-repeated refrain that the poor thing appears to have been pasted together from leftover parts salvaged from the rubbish bin—almost no neck, breast too large, legs too short, tail too small for the oversized breast, eyes too big and set back too far in an overly large and strangely spherical head sporting an oddly long and flexible beak, the upper portion of which is hinged halfway from tip to base as if it had been plucked from the broken beak pile. These descriptions all appear to share the goal of conveying that the woodcock is unsightly, without having to come out and state that directly. To me, that first woodcock I held, as well as each one since, was as beautiful as any bird I'd ever seen. It should be noted that my notion of beauty in the world might skew toward a tail of what many people would call a normal distribution but that I refer to as a Gaussian curve. The gaudy rooster pheasant and splendiferous drake wood duck have their charm but aren't more beautiful than the ruffed grouse dressed in wood tones, with subtle barring and ticking that proclaim, "I am of and for these woods." The unmarked ecru to orange of the woodcock breast is a similar marvel, as are the stubby ebony and ivory tail feathers, contrasted with the woodcock's own variegation along the back. A colleague once suggested that shooting something as stunning as a drake wood duck was almost a crime and I should focus my hunting efforts on things less beautiful, given the special need for beauty in the world. While I am not entirely unsympathetic to some idea buried near the base of that plea, I am certain I couldn't look my reflection in the eye if I were willing to eat bird A and not bird B, simply because bird A's plumage was drabber. Nor could I be content were I only willing to eat a bird raised on a farm rather than one I procured from the wild. But this argument also conflated beauty with showiness and form, instead of function and being. Everything about the way the woodcock is in the world screams "beautiful."

Perhaps the word that best captures the appearance of a woodcock is "bulbous." But if I were limited to a single word to describe these birds, that word might be "under-dense," as unpoetic and maybe non-word-like as that is. In the hand, a wood duck or pheasant is substantial, weighty. The woodcock is startlingly light, its weight all out of proportion to its apparent size, a trick of its bulbosity that adds to the bird's ethereal, ephemeral aura.

Adding to the delight of a timberdoodle, as some call the woodcock, in the hand, is that this bird could have come from anywhere. When I held a grouse, there was a good chance that it had lived its entire life within the range of forest I could see from where I stood, but this little bird might have flown in a few days ago from who knows where. It had all worked out perfectly. My father had been there to share that bird, but I savored the intimacy of the new beginning alone in the woods. Without a doubt, I was enchanted. But there was no way of knowing at that point how important seeing a woodcock each fall would become, how that act would mark the passage of time while it rejuvenated my soul. Life is a single trial experiment. You can't rewind and change the conditions to see how things might work differently as you can with experiments in the lab. I can never know whether woodcock would mean as much to me as they do now if I had shot half a dozen each fall while growing up. Maybe. Or maybe that one bird in that one spot at that one time was exactly what was required to carve a special space in my imagination.

My journey to this moment had been both direct and circuitous, planned and subject to the caroms of chance. The Iowa segment of my life was preceded directly by ten years in northern California, where I was attempting to develop new technology to detect X-rays and gamma-rays, with the hope of distinguishing between neutron stars and black holes in binary systems with stars more like the Sun, stars people think of as "normal." As they age these stars that are more or less like the Sun will expand. If the Sun-like star expands sufficiently, that star's surface material can feel a stronger pull from the nearby black hole or neutron star. When the escaping surface material crashes down toward the neutron star or black hole, it emits X-rays. The question was: Could we build a better detector of those X-rays that would allow us to learn more about the environment that the stellar surface material was falling into?

To pay the bills in the early days of that work, I served as a teaching assistant. My first assignment was instructing students who would rather have nothing to do with physics in the art of solving physics problems and in the laboratory. My recollection, and I am certain I'm not being totally fair in this memory, is that I was trained in the art of teaching by being asked whether I had any questions about teaching. Of course, I had no questions. To have questions I would've had to have thought about the activity for at least a few seconds. My first day in the classroom, however, I stood with students at the board discussing how to productively assess physical situations so that we could make meaning of them, and it was as if a lightbulb went off over my head in cartoon fashion. Whatever I did with the rest of my life, if I could make this activity a central part of it, I would have won the lottery. It was as the 1985 James Burke documentary would have proclaimed, *The Day the Universe Changed*, or certainly the day my universe changed. That moment was re-created when I held that first improbably light and beautiful woodcock in my hand at Old Homestead Place and my universe changed again.

That first day in the classroom probably led more directly to my move to northeast Iowa than did any other single event. As a scientist, my job options were largely in three classes, (1) working at a so-called Research 1 university, with a life built around answering such questions as "What is the nature of the environment around black holes and neutron stars?" (2) working in industry, maybe by sliding fifty miles to the south and riding the Silicon Valley wave; (3) working at an undergraduate college with a focus squarely on teaching. I was advised strongly against the last of these because the jobs were nearly impossible to obtain, and surely I would get bored with the work. It's said that Max Planck's advisor (more than a century ago) advised him against studying physics since it was all but wrapped up and the future lay in chemistry. As the story goes, the advisor claimed that only two minor details remained to be cleaned up in physics—the noninvariance of electromagnetic phenomena under Galilean transformations and the so-called ultraviolet catastrophe in understanding the distribution of different colors of light emitted by hot, dense objects. Planck ignored his advisor and worked out the solution to the ultraviolet catastrophe (surely a bit of hyperbole in the name). His solution to that problem laid the groundwork for Albert Einstein's description of the photoelectric effect and quantum mechanics that would fundamentally and forever change the way we view the world. I paid no more attention to my mentors than did Planck. I pursued the teaching-first option to the extent that I took myself out of consideration for a prestigious postdoctoral scientist appointment that my graduate advisor had opened the door for, before I even had a job offer for any position focused on teaching.

There was, then, a bit riding on the interview I was flying to in northeast Iowa, watching bright comet Hale-Bopp lead me across the country, able to see it against the dark night sky because a crew delay had held our takeoff for hours, meaning I would manage only a few hours of sleep before teaching a class the next morning, one of the key pieces of the interview. That interview day flew by in a blur as the decades have raced by since. Just weeks before the comet guided my way into the future, I'd had dinner with its codiscoverer Thomas Bopp at Alice Waters's now well-known restaurant Chez Panisse. Really bright comets like Hale-Bopp, comets one can walk outside and look up to say "Wow" at, occur maybe every twenty years on average. This one was the second of my life, the second in as many years. As part of my work as an education and outreach scientist for the Center for Particle Astrophysics, I'd observed the earlier Comet Hyakutake with the residents of the Manchester–Point Arena Rancheria in Mendocino County, California. Comets have two tails. The dust tail shines white from reflected sunlight, and it curves back toward the comet's orbital path. The gas tail glows blue and points straight away from the Sun. Hale-Bopp had splendid examples of each tail. Comet Hyakutake had almost no dust tail, but oh that wondrous gas tail filling the dark Point Arena sky! Earlier in the night, we had observed Venus through a telescope, and a more senior gentleman remarked, "It looks like the Moon!" Venus goes through a complete set of phases, new when on the same side of the Sun as us, transitioning through first quarter to full as its orbit carries it to the side of the Sun opposite us. Over the first two decades of the seventeenth century, Johannes Kepler developed a set of mathematical laws that described beautifully the observed motions of the planets, Kepler's laws forming a scientific model of not only our solar system but the bedrock on which our understanding of the entire universe would eventually rest. Kepler's mathematically precise model demanded that Venus be just over six times farther away from us at its greatest distance when it is on the far side of the Sun than it is at its closest point on the near side of the Sun. It is a well-known fact that objects of fixed size, like Venus's diameter, appear larger when closer and smaller at greater distances. Perhaps less well known is that the relationship between apparent size ("angular size" astronomers might say) and distance is linear. Sometimes human beings have a seemingly hardwired tendency to treat all relationships as linear, and it can get us in trouble. But it works here, since an object appears two times smaller when it is twice as far away, three times smaller when three times more distant and so on. That Venus appears about six times smaller when nearly full than it does when nearly new is remarkable observational evidence in support of the Copernican-Keplerian heliocentric model. After a long evening of our observing the heavens together, the young men of the community broke into dance and song, conferring on me a Pomo name that translated to English (so I was told) as Big Eye, referring to my telescope. It was a night of educational transcendence that would make it all but impossible to accept a job designed to force me to be so focused on the lab that there would be no time for any teaching of any sort.

Those two comets worked their magic, and I landed in a nearly ideal job in a nearly ideal setting, where I remain, with dark skies above, the big river a mere forty miles to the east, Minnesota fifteen miles to the north, and the sporadic edge of prairie potholes an easy drive to the west. It's hard to imagine a place more suited to my outdoor leanings, with all manner of fish and game mingling where forest, prairie, rivers, trout streams, and lakes meet in the heart of one of the continent's major waterfowl flyways. It's just as hard to imagine a place more suited to my drive to study the heavens and discuss the universe with the world. I fell quickly into a rhythm in which every day that I walked into the classroom or the planetarium or the observatory, there was no place I would rather be and nothing I would rather be doing than talking about whatever slice of the universe was our topic for that day with whatever slice of humanity was in the room at the time. Just as quickly, I became what is known as a rough shooter, wandering far and wide for the opportunity to hunt whatever birds crossed my path. I relished the evolution of autumn, as the passing weeks turned my focus from rails and snipe to wood ducks, then pheasants, followed by ruffed grouse, turkeys, and late-season ducks. Somewhere in there, the time, maybe just a day, would be right for woodcock. And woodcock rose to the pinnacle of my bird-hunting pyramid, even though I rarely shot more than one per year and have never shot more than two, one or two always being enough to fill my need to hold them. Every bird I down and hold in my hand touches my soul, but something about those woodcock over the years touched my soul in a distinctly deeper way.

My journals record twenty-three woodcock bagged in the past twenty-two years. For the recent third of that span the allure of woodcock has grown as I have been part of the United States Fish and Wildlife Service (USFWS) Wing Survey. Last year, I submitted one of the two woodcock wings from the state of Iowa. October 10 is the earliest I

have bagged a woodcock in a year and November 17 is the latest, with most coming during the last week of October or the first week of November. Three years, I have failed to get a woodcock; four years, I bagged two; the remaining fifteen years produced a single woodcock. During my twenty-two years of Iowa woodcock, I have taken birds from eight different properties, all public. Four of these properties have produced a single woodcock, and the most productive property has produced seven. There are a few spots where I have fallen into the bad habit of expecting to find birds year after year.

Time has done what time will do. Ruffed grouse are all but gone from Iowa, if not entirely gone, with doves now making up a portion of each fall's time afield. The turkeys are on a down part of a cycle, at least we hope it's a cycle and not a trend. Deer are ascendant. Bow hunters swarm over our bird covers. My legs don't want the all-day hunts they once did. Through all the change, that one woodcock has remained the most essential part of each autumn afield. T. S. Eliot's Prufrock noted, "I have measured out my life with coffee spoons." It would be hard to argue with the notion that I have measured out my life with the coming and going of familiar stars, but surely I have also measured out my life with the coming and going of woodcock, learning more about stars and woodcock with every passing year, yet ever more and more perplexed by celestial objects and birds alike, my appreciation of the beauty of each continuously expanding. Whether in the end these measures have more meaning than coffee spoons or not is, I suppose, a matter of debate.

YEAR 2

Trusting the Process

In a manner that I couldn't possibly fathom at the time, that first Old Homestead Place woodcock was critically important in anchoring me to my new home, a marker of place, surely, because there are no woodcock any meaningful distance west of where I landed, and a marker of time because these birds were foreign to me in my youth. But the bird was more than a mere signpost signaling "you are here and now instead of there and then." No, it said something more like "I will bind you to the earth here and remind you of the sky above, ensuring you understand this is your home, a home stretching beyond this physical place, to a community that understands what it means to make some sort of living from the wildness around, and a home with those who study the world, using data to build models of the universe." Tycho Brahe is an important reminder of that last place I call home.

With a plan to study law, Tycho Brahe matriculated at the University of Copenhagen in 1559, eighty years after the university's opening. He would be essential to Kepler's work in building a precise mathematical model of the solar system, but he would be just as essential in helping create what we call "science" today. As I routinely tell my students that if one is not careful, it is possible to fall in with the wrong crowd at college, and so it was with Brahe when he began hanging around the astronomers. The list of ways I feel a connection with Brahe is long. When I work hard to teach the basic structure as well as the nuances of the practice of science, I rely heavily on Brahe's practically perfecting the concept of rigorously testing hypotheses' predictions. As I focused my graduate school research on attempting to build novel instrumentation for making improved measurements of the heavens, I was emulating Brahe. I can trace part of my need to build a statistical understanding of the entirety of existence to Brahe's insistence on measuring a single quantity multiple times with multiple instruments. At a pivotal moment in his career, Brahe observed a bright comet, just as I would. I've poked around a little to see whether Brahe was a hunter but haven't turned up anything other than the common recognition that he was born into an aristocratic life that surely would have included some form of hunting, albeit likely something I might not even recognize as hunting. My office has artwork adorning the walls and surfaces. There's a print of a ruffed grouse, a print of Andrew Wyeth's *Coot Hunter*, a photograph of Comet Hale-Bopp, and a print of a schematic from the planetarium patent application. The only images of real-to-life beings are two photographs of dogs that have graced my life and a print of a portrait of Tycho Brahe. I don't go out of my way to point this fact out to my wife, Kristin.

Brahe was an expert at measuring in general and measuring parallax specifically. Parallax is the apparent shifting of foreground objects against a distant backdrop when viewed from different positions. If you hold your upright thumb in front of your face and blink your eyes, alternately closing left and right, your thumb appears to jump back and forth. That's parallax. The more distant the nearby object, the less it shifts against the background. You can demonstrate this by moving your thumb from just a few inches in front of your nose out to arm's length and back, all while blinking left and right. I prefer to think about my appearance to a crossing woodcock as I stand motionless in the forest; when seen against the background forest by the flying woodcock, I look to be moving the opposite direction from the bird's motion. The bird records my image shifting against the distant trees. If the bird flushed a few yards out, providing a shot that even I can sometimes make, then the bird sees my image sliding rapidly against the distant forest. The woodcock who says, "Maybe today's not your day," flushing at a distance of forty yards, sees me sliding much more slowly against the background forest, despite each bird's flying at the same rate. Measuring how much an object appears to shift when viewed from two different locations of known separation will, with an application of trigonometry, yield the object's distance. For astronomers those two different observation points could be widely separated locations on Earth or different points along Earth's orbit. Brahe understood this concept maybe more deeply than anyone before him. Perhaps he had even generalized the idea to an understanding of the value of looking at all things from different perspectives. Perhaps he hadn't. However much the practice of measuring parallax had fueled a philosophy of life for Brahe, when a bright comet appeared in 1577, he was more than ready to use parallax measurements to show that the comet lay well beyond the Moon, dashing a previously held belief that comets were atmospheric phenomena.

At the time Brahe observed the comet, the two leading models for how the universe worked were Copernicus's idea that had planets circling the Sun and Ptolemy's system, developed 1,400 years before Copernicus and built on objects circling Earth. These "circlings" were achieved by means of nested glass spheres rotating around either Earth or the Sun, the apparently nonsensical idea of space being filled with invisible forces (gravity) not yet having taken root. In the Ptolemaic model, these glass spheres spun around Earth at the bottom, causing all celestial objects to move across our sky at rates tied to the spinning speeds of the spheres to which they were attached. In the Copernican model, the Sun is moved to the heart of the nested spheres, while Earth resides on one of the moving spheres. One is tempted to say that *the* problem confronting each model was that of retrograde motion, but usually it's better to think about *a* problem or *an* issue with any idea, since many different things might be causing troubles at once. Because any one of those things might simultaneously cause problems and be useful, maybe it's best to avoid thinking about these things as problems exactly.

Still, retrograde motion needed to be explained. Most of the time, careful observation reveals that on any given night a planet appears just east of where it was the night before when measured against some star. Every now and then, life gets interesting and a planet reverses direction. For a while the planet appears farther west against the stars each night. Ptolemy attempted to account for this phenomenon by having the planets attached to smaller glass spheres. These smaller spheres were attached to and spinning independently from the larger glass spheres. That extra spinning could sometimes make a planet appear to hit reverse. Copernicus posited his model, largely because it provided a seemingly simpler explanation for retrograde motion. If we were catching up and passing the outer planets, it would lead them to only appear to be moving backward against the stars, much like a car we are passing on the highway appears to be moving backward against the distant hills, although we know it is traveling the same direction we are. This outcome is another example of parallax as our observation vantage point moves from "behind" the car (or planet) to in front of the car (or planet).

Early in his budding astronomical career, Brahe had observed a conjunction of Saturn and Jupiter when they passed like ships—well, planets—in the night, their separation on our sky shrinking to its smallest before opening back up. These two brightest of the outer planets have such a passing about every twenty years, and it would have been an event of monumental importance to astrologers of Brahe's time. Thus, many people would have been using the models of Ptolemy and Copernicus to predict the timing of the big event. When Brahe found that predictions based on Copernican models were up to ten times closer to the actual time of conjunction than were predictions made based on Ptolemaic models, he made a decision that was critical for the development of science. Many people would have declared Copernicus the winner and moved on. When Brahe recognized that they were both wrong and there was no winner, I envision him saying

"*&!@!!#%^&&!!@!#!"—in Danish or maybe Latin, of course. Having decided that neither model was sufficient, Brahe deduced, correctly, that only better data from improved observations would lead to a truer understanding of the geometry of our part of the universe. The decision to toss out both models and make improved measurements can be seen as a sort of cornerstone on which science is built. More than anything else, science is a process, a way of doing things that hinges on careful observational tests of models. Picture the scientific process as a never-ending loop, like the track at the Indianapolis Motor Speedway or the orbit of Earth or the coming and going of woodcock and other birds with the passing of the seasons. The loop of science has key locales around the circuit: we use our current knowledge to make a model of the way things work; to be scientific, that model must make a prediction of something that is observable, like the timing of a conjunction of Saturn and Jupiter. Then we test the model by observing; if the prediction is experimentally confirmed, within the uncertainty of the test, we don't say the model is proven true, just that it passed this particular test. If the observational test finds something different from what was predicted, we do say that the model was falsified (with the caveat that sometimes we make errors in interpreting data) and that the model must be discarded or modified. Just because a model passes one observational test, we don't stop testing it. Picture it as if walking around our track repeatedly, never reaching the finish line. Make an observation. Is the observation consistent with what the model predicted? Modify the model as needed. Predict. Observe. Repeat. Eventually, we walk less actively around a given track after the model on that track has been tested repeatedly, but we always know some surprise could upend the model at any point. With a single observation of the conjunction of Jupiter and Saturn, Brahe falsified two models.

To provide the improved data set needed, Brahe devoted more than two decades of his life to observing the positions of the planets against the background stars, with ever-improving accuracy and precision. Accuracy refers to how close the average observed value is to the actual value, while precision can be thought of as the spread of a group of measurements. Picture five arrows sent downrange to a target. Accuracy is a measure of how close the average position of those arrows is to the bullseye; precision refers to the spread in individual arrow positions—how tight the group is, in the language of shooters. Brahe improved both accuracy and precision for planetary positions by measuring multiple times with multiple instruments and fretting over those instruments, never fully trusting what they were telling him. The result was a staggering improvement over anything that had come earlier, a data set that was up to the task of discerning what modifications to the model of Copernicus were required.

Before the end of 1599, after an upheaval in the royal family that had sponsored his work, Brahe had moved from Denmark to Prague, where Johannes Kepler joined him less than a year later. As good an observer as Brahe was, and he was the best the world had ever known, he was not up to solving the immense geometry problem of extracting a physical model from his mountains of data. Kepler, mathematician extraordinaire, was the right person for that job. By all accounts it was a match made, if not in hell, certainly not in heaven. Brahe was flamboyant, luxuriating in the glow of the royal court. Kepler was serious, maybe we would even say dour, wanting nothing more than to work on the hardest math problem of the day. Holding both the power and the data, Brahe chose to share little with Kepler. The relationship was bitter, but the story astronomers pass on to each new generation of young astronomers is that as he lay dying, Brahe's final words were directed not to his family but to Kepler. He asked Kepler, finally, to make something meaningful out of his life's work of measuring the planets. The story goes on to say that Brahe's family was no more forthcoming with the data than Brahe himself had been, forcing Kepler to steal the data and leave town.

Kepler spent year after year using Brahe's data to work on a single math problem, deducing the laws of planetary motion that bear his name. He showed that Brahe's observations were consistent with planets orbiting the Sun, though with noncircular, elliptical orbits. Ellipses are like flattened circles with one axis longer than the other. He also demonstrated that the planets sped up in a precise way when closer to the Sun and that there was a specific mathematical relationship between how far a planet was from the Sun and time it took to complete an orbit around the Sun. We are now in a position to see the true beauty of the process of science in action. The model of the solar system based on Kepler's laws predicts that a nearly new, slender crescent Venus, like I had the immense honor of sharing a view of with the people in the Manchester–Point Arena Rancheria community, must be about six times larger than a nearly full Venus. When Galileo trained his telescope on Venus, it was this very precise size-phase relationship that he confirmed. Over the centuries, Kepler's model has needed to be extended and refined in detail, but it has passed the major observational tests.

The work of Copernicus, Brahe, Kepler, and Galileo showed that the solar system is large, with vast amounts of empty space between the planets orbiting the Sun. It was, of course, just the first tiny step in our understanding of the size of the universe, with nearly unfathomable stretches of space between stars in our Galaxy and even greater stretches of space separating one galaxy from another, but it was a first step that provided us with a real sense of where we are. It provided me with a sort of spiritual home because I was drawn to this way of understanding the world around me. It shaped even my encounters with fish and game, underpinning the connection I felt to something larger and grander when I encountered woodcock in my new physical home.

The year following my first woodcock, while exploring the woods and fields that now formed my home, making and testing predictions however explicitly or implicitly, I found what would become my most productive go-to woodcock covert. It was a narrow strip of forest lining a creek bed that was usually dry but sometimes held water that flowed into a nearby trout stream. This draw sported low brush and timber, along with a tangle of downed trees from the occasional spring flood. The stretch is about a quarter of a mile long, but another shorter run of good edge cover joins it at a right angle at one point. Year after year, I find woodcock somewhere in this cover, with the result that this is the property that has produced more birds than any other. I try not to hunt it much every year. It's just that special. We'll refer to this property as Arroyo Place.

Just as he had been when that first woodcock flew a year earlier, my father was with me again for the discovery of Arroyo Place. We had sneaked out for a quick pheasant hunt after work one day and were chatting our way back to the truck. Pheasant shooting ends at 4:30 in Iowa, never mind when sunset is, meaning we found ourselves past legal pheasant shooting time with twenty minutes or so remaining before the end of legal shooting for most everything else. When we reached the arroyo, my dad waited in the trail as I wandered up the draw to see if there was any sign of woodcock. About fifty yards in, a woodcock flushed while I was thoroughly unprepared, even though flushing a woodcock had been exactly what I was trying to do. With the bird having flown a good distance, darkness growing steadily, and with my father standing back at the trail, having hunted enough for the afternoon, I mulled over whether to give chase. As I pondered, a second woodcock came up from pretty much the exact same spot as the first. I missed cleanly and efficiently despite it being a wide-open shot. It is not atypical for me to miss the first shot at a woodcock in any year and often the second. It didn't help that I had a tight pheasant choke in the gun, which hadn't allowed much spread before the shot reached the distance of the bird. As I strolled back to meet my dad, I stored away not just where these birds had been but the exhilaration I felt when they flushed.

Dad still wasn't sure woodcock were gamebirds at all, let alone birds worth spending time and energy chasing through the thickest cover around, when grouse and pheasants were plentiful. So for the next few days while he was still in town, we turned our attention elsewhere. After my parents' departure, work intervened, and it was a couple more weeks before I got out again. It was, in fact, one day before the end of the woodcock season in mid-November.

As I have regularly since, I returned to my newfound arroyo, walking all the way to the end of the wash and returning, basically retracing my steps, when a woodcock flushed and I missed again. To be fair, this was a much more challenging shot, with the bird offering mere glimpses through the cover. I was headed toward the spot where I marked the bird down when it flushed wilder this time, and I missed another challenging shot, certain I had marked it down yet again. Despite what you might have been led to believe, the third time is not always the charm—the bird flushed very wild, offering only the sound of its wings. Back at the truck, I decided to close out the woodcock season at the property where I got my first bird, Old Homestead Place, but at a location distant from the old homestead.

I was mostly hunting pheasants now, cutting a long path through prairie grass and along a cornfield, flushing a couple of hens along the way. My energy was more or less boundless in those days, so when I got to the end of this trek, I thought "Well, why not follow this farmer's road a mile down the hill to a clear-cut?" Switching to a grouse-friendly set-up of looser choke and lighter loads, I entered the small cut, working it thoroughly. No grouse were home that day, and I popped out on the farmer's road with a slender strip of cover across the road from the clear-cut. A narrow entrance road, carved through this dense cover, led to an open field beyond the strip of young trees. Figuring it was worth checking to see if the grass in the field looked like pheasant cover, I walked the entrance road, brush encroaching from right and left, when a woodcock came out of the grass, flying straight away. This shot resulted in my second woodcock in as many years. As I bent to gather my bird, another woodcock flushed from the grass beside the fallen bird. Content with one bird to end the season, I let the second one fly without offering a shot.

In the story "Forty-Crook Branch," Tom Kelly wrote, "If you happen to hunt a great deal, or if you spend a lot of time in the woods for any other reason, there always seems to be a half-section of land, somewhere, that fits you better than it fits anybody else." Kelly adds, "It could be an outcropping of rock, maybe a special view, or perhaps a stand of trees, but it seems that you never go to that place without the distinct feeling that you are coming home." So it was with me and Old Homestead Place in these early days, the half-section being used loosely to refer to a sweet spot, a honey hole of any size. Things have evolved, and other half-sections have joined and maybe supplanted Old Homestead Place as locations that most elicit that coming-home feeling. Of course, we can stretch the definition of "half-section of land" to recognize a homecoming in a certain patch of night sky or a favored classroom or the process of science itself, some of us equating a successful life's journey with finding these homes.

Back at the parking lot on the day of my second-ever woodcock, I found a conservation officer grilling an out-of-state deer hunter. He paused his harangue to ask for my license and did a bag check, the only time I have ever had a bag check in more than forty years of hunting. We talked a bit about woodcock, the out-of-state hunter deriding the worthless little birds, before the conservation officer returned his attention to the deer hunter, who must have seemed suspect in some way. They were still fully engaged when I drove away. After that day, usually at Old Homestead Place, I encountered that same conservation officer regularly. He never asked to see what was in my bag again but always wanted to know what all I had seen in the miles and miles I walked across those hills. Sometimes he would tell me a bit about his day; sometimes he wouldn't. I began to believe he recognized my truck and, whenever feasible, he waited around or circled back to catch me for a chat as I reappeared in the lot. Eventually, I thought of him as a friend, wondering how he was doing, what misadventures he was embroiled in, whenever a few autumn months slipped past without our encountering one another. He retired, likely a dozen years ago, given how way has led on to way. I've never met his successor.

YEAR 3
Wheels Rolling

Don't tell anyone this, because it's a secret we wouldn't want to get out, but one of my favorite pastimes is sitting in meetings waiting for somebody to say, "There's no need to reinvent the wheel." Is it possible, I wonder, to look at a modern wheel and believe that it hasn't been fundamentally reinvented again and again? Imagine trying to drive your fancy new car down the highway on a wheel from 1400 or 1880 or 1920 or even, really, 1950. What would the world be like if, after the first wheel came into existence, nobody ever said, "You know, I think we can make that better." Before I know it, my mind is picturing those ubiquitous cartoon images of prehistoric people chipping the first wheels out of stone. I get lost thinking about where we might be if nobody had ever tried to reinvent the wheel, while the meeting has moved on without me, so much the better in all likelihood.

The metaphor of much of life as a wheel is pretty common. Once I wrote a blog post titled "Wheel in the Sky Keeps on Turning, Pretty Sure Where I'll Be Tomorrow" to explore my penchant for finding a home and settling into it. We can pause for those of you unfamiliar with the band Journey to look that one up. Key here is that the wheels of life don't spin futilely in one place but roll along so that not only is the wheel in a different place after one rotation but it wears with each rotation so that it is not exactly the same wheel. Each autumn, I am back in the classroom teaching students the beauty of the universe and, in particular, the beauty of the human effort to understand the universe. It feels as if it should be the same as the year before, but I have changed, the students are different, and we have new knowledge of the universe. Each autumn, I am back in the woodcock woods hunting those few birds that have summered locally and the many more that migrate through, heading to Louisiana or thereabouts, having nested or been reared to the north. Once again, the wheel has rolled and I am different, the birds are different, and the forest has evolved.

Where others build a Thanksgiving meal around a much larger bird, Kristin and I devote energy to planning something special with a woodcock course. Once upon a time, that was rumaki, a favorite of ours, made following a recipe from *Game Bird Cookery*, although now we typically make it with rail or snipe. Dressing and cooking birds I have shot is an important ritualistic part of each passing autumn, as vital a part of the hunting experience as shooting the bird in the first place. While it would not have been the case twenty years ago, I am now no longer certain eating animals would remain part of my life without this opportunity to watch a bird die, a bird that had every intention to live, as a result of my actions. That brief sense of loss, of recognition of what I have done to remove a beautiful breathing member of the community of all living things, makes the times I didn't take ownership for killing what I ate at least somewhat more acceptable. Of course, it's not only about eating. There's very little we do in the modern world, from turning on a light switch to getting dressed, that doesn't involve loss and death somewhere along the line. My taking the life of a bird with the attendant opportunity to give thanks to the universe at every step of the process serves as a sort of sacrament, absolving me, to a degree, of some of my carelessness in not giving a second thought to the birds that died to yield the boneless thighs that get plunked into the slow cooker. From the moment I first kneel over the bird and discern what it had been eating, to admiring the liver, pulmonary, renal, and cardiovascular systems, I feel the stain of my careless interactions with the world washing away. This absolution continues all the way through careful planning, preparing, and eating a meal centered on that bird. I haven't studied the topic thoroughly, but it strikes me that for my entire existence, Americans have more or less imagined themselves as apart from the natural world, something entirely different from the world around. All that has really changed in my nearly six decades is our ability to live that reality more and more, to the detriment of the world and ourselves. It has been my great fortune to have the opportunity to resist that tide and craft a life of living close to the land, reminded repeatedly of the oneness of existence.

The entire operation of putting in the time to locate birds and turn them into food provides a much deeper bond to the world as well. When I eat a woodcock, some of the carbon from fat and protein in the bird is used in my cells, becoming part of me. The woodcock got that carbon from earthworms, which in turn, got the carbon from soil, and soil got the carbon from all sorts of different things, including but not limited to decaying plant roots, limbs, and leaves. The carbon dioxide I exhale is absorbed by the leaves of plants, thus returning some of the carbon I ingested back to the world around, enabling the process to start anew, or more accurately, to roll on. This carbon cycle, a wheel rolling ever forward, has been active for as long as there has been life on Earth, the carbon shared among all living things that are and have been and will be. Earth gets no new carbon, having only what it was formed with 4.6 billion years ago. I dream that it would be possible once my story ends to be left to return my nutrients to the soil of some dense willow stand by a bog, directly feeding the worms that will feed the woodcock that have fed my body and spirit for these many years. I am reminded of a student presentation years ago during which the student shared that he grew up on a cattle farm hearing his father tell the cattle, "I'll feed you and you'll feed me." My heart wants to whisper the same to the woodcock but in reverse, "You woodcock will feed me and I will feed you woodcock."

In recent years I have had opportunities to confront my mortality and to consider how the opportunity to feed woodcock has always been near and grows ever-nearer. In the days when I was first encountering northeast Iowa woodcock, I'd only had brushes with such opportunities, seen vaguely through a watery lens. In addition to a few incidents related to driving my car too fast on country roads as a teenager, there was a flu I had in graduate school. I was so sick that I couldn't stand up for two days, fever burning me up. But I was young, possessing a youthful and unconscious misconception of invincibility and largely unaware of the serious nature of such infections, or even really the difference between a cold and the flu. In retrospect, surely I should have gone to the hospital, but I don't think antivirals were much of a thing then and maybe not much could have been done. Had I closed my eyes and attuned my ears, I might have heard the distant—or not so distant—flutter of the wings of the angel of death.

I had a hospital stay encompassing the days leading up to my twenty-first birthday. Growing up, I'd had tonsillitis on a regular basis. It knocked me down for a few days each time after an onset, marked most frequently, interestingly enough, by aching calf muscles. We were in a phase of not extracting tonsils at that point. I've no idea where we are now in that cycle but then I was told, "You would get colds and be just as sick just as frequently; the tonsils have nothing to do with this" and "You will grow out of this." These are among the great falsehoods foisted on me during my youth. After my tonsils were removed, my frequency of cold or flu acquisition was cut by a factor of five, and the severity of illness was diminished by an even greater factor. By the time I was in high school, my tonsils were permanently twice normal size and craggy so that they could make an unsuspecting new physician recoil in horror with a glance at my throat. The bottom fell out on me during the spring semester of my junior year in college, tonsillitis arriving in January and never going away. First, I took penicillin, then ampicillin, followed by erythromycin and Keflex. Absent improvement, we decided, "Hey, let's cycle through them again." Times were different, and I would make other choices today.

By April it was clear things were not getting better for me, neither the infection in the tonsils nor my irritable bowel syndrome that was raging with all those antibiotics, and we decided that I would take incompletes in my courses and the tonsils would finally come out. I checked into the hospital early in an attempt to get my white blood count up, since it was lower than my ENT surgeon felt was safe for surgery. Several days later, when the white blood count adhered resolutely to that low level, he told me that we needed to go ahead with the operation and it wasn't really a problem, but his face wasn't exactly selling this new approach. Recovery was slow and my GI system never did fully bounce back. It's impossible to know just how near the wings of the angel of death were throughout this encounter but likely closer than I imagined at the time.

Since that first Old Homestead Place encounter, no year has passed without offering at least something of a chance at gathering a woodcock to partake of its carbon, however meager that chance. In the year that followed my second Old Homestead Place bird, the only opportunity was pretty meager.

In these early years, my hunting always began with a five-day early duck season in late September. I used the first day of that season as my chance to get started on the year as well as an opportunity to scout for grouse. Parking at the top of the hill at Old Homestead Place, I would pick my way down to the creek in full darkness. After a couple of hours of posting for a pass shooting opportunity and then hole jumping for wood ducks, I would meander the long way back to the top, looking and listening for signs of grouse. As much as I preferred other forms of hunting for other birds, this was the best day of the year. Because it had been so long time since any hunting, I barely slept the night before, more like a thirteen-year-old than the mature adult I was.

When hiking down the hill, I would pause after turning a particular corner on the trail, exposed limestone bluff towering over me as the first sounds of the rippling trout stream drifted up from below. Some years, I could hear the woodies making all sorts of noise as they were rising for the day; other years, as with this one, all was quiet. Jumping no birds on approach, I leaned against a tree along one leg of a large U bend, a deeper hole to my right at the base of the U and a deeper hole to my left at the top of one leg of the U. The wait was a short few minutes. A group of five woodies whistled around the corner, moving left to right. Firmly out of character, I was ready instead of lost in a dream about carbon cycles and such. I drew on the lead bird and dropped it cleanly with a solid splash in the shallow riffles directly in front of me. To my dismay, a bird well back in the middle of the flock also angled out and fell with a thud on the far bank, an unwanted "two birds with one stone" (the stone being a two-and-three-quarter-inch-high brass #4 steel shotgun shell for the overly literal among you) situation. You see, the limit was two wood ducks in those days, meaning my opening day was over. I had planned to shoot one bird early if the fates were so inclined, saving the other spot in my bag for a couple hours of enjoyable poking along the creek. It must have been a heck of a flyer, the single pellet that dropped the bird trailing so far behind the lead duck. Remarkably, both birds were dead in the air. In retrospect, this start should have been a clear sign that this would be a different kind of year.

As for the lone appearance of a woodcock this year, it happened on a road trip to central Wisconsin with, once again, my dad. As an aside, I have learned much in this effort to recount the tale of my life with woodcock. Before this effort, I had believed that my father was a peripheral character in the narrative, having never shot a woodcock himself and never really quite taken to the birds as game. Yet as I read my journals and dredge up the memories, there he is at every seminal moment in the early days. Six months ago, as I write this, my mother finally moved into long-term care, where she is immobile and largely but not wholly uncommunicative. Parkinson's disease has effectively won the battle, as it was always destined to do. She should have moved much earlier, but my father wouldn't hear of it, insisting on being her primary caregiver despite his own frailty. Every time they met a new healthcare provider in those later days, the provider would ask who cared for mother at home, and the answer of my father clearly led to them thinking, "This can't possibly be so." Now he is alone in the house where I grew up, alone for the first time in all of his eighty-five years. I talk to him on the phone twice a day, but there is little to talk about, no real conversation, unless I can recount a hunting or fishing outing and he tries to untangle one location from another in his memory, often asking, "Is that where we . . . ?"

This particular fall, my dad and I decided to make a quick road trip to see what central Wisconsin held for us, driving as far as I could manage, leaving after a full day of work at the end of a full week of work. We'd hunt all day the next day and then drive home, stopping along the way to hunt here and there as we liked. Getting farther into northern Wisconsin would have meant more grouse but more time behind the wheel and less time walking new country. We opted to maximize time in the field, figuring Iowa grouse hunting was going so well that any distance north into Wisconsin would surely be sufficient to provide some chances at birds. It was to be the only hunting road trip my dad and I would ever make together.

We hopped from one spot that looked promising on a map to another, hiking awhile before deciding whether to stick with this locale or find another spot. In many places the cover looked great but, predictably, given the newness of the area and the limited time we had to figure it out, flushes were scarce. In fact, we flushed all of one bird, a woodcock that got up three times in front of my dad as we worked down a long brush row with open fields to either side. This was his chance to be won over to woodcock, but it never quite clicked on any of those flushes. On the last one, the bird swung my direction after a bit of flying straight away from my dad. I took a shot that was pretty far out there for my skeet choke, but the bird flew on. That was my lone look at a woodcock for the year. As for my dad, I don't think the woodcock was the highlight of the trip. Instead, it was all the cranberry bogs we drove past as we headed home, while he speculated on how various aspects of the cranberry farming operation might get completed. Finally, we stopped at one of the farms and purchased what appeared to me to be a lifetime supply of the fruit. For years afterward, he talked about seeing those operations, and if I mention that trip on the phone today, the conversation turns to cranberries.

Despite my failing to bag a woodcock, it was a bountiful year, when possibilities seemed endless. One could see the forests and fields full of birds stretching into an infinite future. Before that trip to Wisconsin, I had shot two ruffed grouse on two shots, a most unlikely occurrence. The first came on a property that stretches along the river, the limestone bluffs even steeper than by many of the nearby trout streams, a property we will get to know as Spring Fish Place. Clinging to the side of one of those bluffs, I sent a grouse uphill in front of me. Knowing that the bird would likely want to get back downhill toward where it first flushed, I circled around to put myself directly between where it had flown and where it had started before I crept gingerly up the hill. The bird exploded and flew directly over my head while I had one foot a good eighteen inches higher up the hill than the other. I swung as hard as I could, tumbling the bird in a puff of feathers as I tumbled myself in an awkward fall.

A week later, I was side-hilling just above a trout stream when a grouse blasted out of thick brush beneath some cedars, headed for the stream. My gun was up and firing in an instant, but still the bird disappeared as I pulled the trigger. I didn't see it fall behind the screen of cover, but something about the silence told me it was down. It lay out in the open, light breast feathers pointed skyward.

My last grouse of the year came on New Year's Day, after I'd flushed at least five different birds on New Year's Eve. To those who hunt the North Woods, this level of grouse activity must seem sparse, but it felt like a massive wave in Iowa. This year's three is the most I ever shot in a season, and I'd seen so many more. We were awash in grouse. Just a few years later, they were getting hard to find, and a half dozen years after that, they were all but gone. In addition to the grouse and the ducks, beautiful pheasants filled the fields, and pheasant graced every holiday table that year. After a weather-induced crash, the pheasant population rebounded, but never near the level of this year.

The most memorable bird of the season came when I was visiting my parents a few days before Christmas, back in the land where my hunting life had started. In the long-ago days, we usually hunted the hill above where my father grew up, sweeping a large circle above the house and garden, dropping back down to the barn on the other end of the property, deep in the valley below the hilltop property of my mother's youth. The barn sat near the potato patch, where we would gather to plant each spring and harvest each fall, the potatoes meant to feed the entire extended family all winter. So precious were they that when a hard freeze threatened, someone stayed up watching the heater in the root cellar, attempting to ensure the crop didn't freeze. All my aunts, uncles, and cousins would gather for the harvest—not that gathering meant much travel. I was the first in my generation or the one before to leave a three-county area. When we dug the potatoes, my grandfather would drive the tractor and my dad, being the oldest child, would stand atop the plow, forcing it to dig deeper, rolling red and gold treasure to the surface. The rest of us followed behind, some knocking dirt off the spuds and gathering them into piles for others to put into buckets. Still others carried the buckets to the wagon, where they awaited the trip to the root cellar.

The land that was in my mom's family, the property containing what we call Grandpa Place, has a different character in my memory than does the property that was in my dad's family, likely in part because I knew my mom's parents less well, both of them having passed away before I reached eighth grade. Both of my dad's parents lived until I was an adult, allowing me to get to know them and their interaction with the land, employing an adult's eyes and experience. But the properties are different. The valley where my dad grew up has richer soil and is protected from the wind that always seemed to be blowing atop the hill where my mom was raised on the thinner soil. Even in my childish naïveté I could sense how much harder the living had to be on top of the hill, how one felt nearer some edge. When I was younger, I decried all the effort my parents expended mowing vast swaths of grass on that land, using time and money to rob quail of habitat, but I get it. The clean, manicured landscape fed the illusion that the dark edge of oblivion had been pushed a bit farther away.

Two fishing ponds adorned the property of my mother's family. Well, in my mind they were fishing ponds, although at least one of them was likely built as a cattle-watering pond. That cattle pond was a tiny half-acre puddle on the part of the property that my parents later owned. A newer, four-times-bigger pond sat on the property where my uncle lived. It was just up the road toward the little church carved out of the woods on land my mom's family had donated. These ponds were formative for me. My earliest memories of the land include my grandfather giving me his best cane pole when we were bluegill fishing the pond. He said, "Now hang on tight. I don't want to lose that pole." I was maybe four, so the first thing I did when a sizable fish took my bait was let the pole slip from my hands while my grandfather laughed and laughed, his best pole racing around the surface of the pond that, a year or so later, would produce my first real bass. That bass was a three pounder, a fish bigger than my imagination could hold. Years later, I stood transfixed at the edge of that small pond, watching a male largemouth bass nudge around a female bass twice his size, tilting up to spread milt on the eggs she was depositing, before finally pushing her away toward deeper water to keep her from eating the freshly fertilized eggs. Once, while I was casting from the dam, a snake suddenly appeared, as if a helix had been fired from a gun. It captured a sizable sunfish, turning the fish to be swallowed headfirst, the platter-like panfish creating a bulge in the snake worthy of a cartoon serpent. Muskrats proved an existential threat to the pond by carving numerous hollows and runs in the dam, creating an open lattice within the solid structure. My dad thought we'd save the pond by his stomping on a den while I stood over the underwater entrance with a .22 handgun. My task was to shoot the muskrat missile as it ejected from its home, something akin to attempting to catch a full-speed pass from an NFL quarterback standing five feet away, with a screen shielding the ball from view until it is a foot away. My dad must have thought I was some kind of magician. Had I ever managed to hit a muskrat, I'm not sure that gun would have done much damage.

The very best fish of my younger days, a five-and-three-quarter-pound largemouth, came from the larger pond down the road when I was fifteen or sixteen. We were spending the weekend at the old mobile home, our cabin in the country, on the property where my mom's parents had last lived. On this sweltering Saturday in late May, my mother delivered me to a creek in the Hoosier National Forest, dropping me at a bridge, with a plan to retrieve me at the next bridge ten hours later, after I'd caught scores, if not hundreds, of bluegill, bass, and crappie. After waving my mother away, I busted heavy brush down to the creek, where I discovered that somehow, somewhere, the handle had backed off my spinning reel, forever lost. I made one feeble cast, handlining the lure back. Only two choices presented themselves: walk to the other bridge and sit in its shade for nine hours until my ride arrived or walk the seven miles to my dad's parents' house under the blazing Sun while dressed for busting heavy cover.

Given my inability to sit still under ideal conditions, there really was no choice to be made. Ninety percent of the walk was along a state highway that was not terribly heavily traveled, although it was nothing but blind curves with rises and dips, such that traffic from the front or rear had no chance to see me before they were right on top of me and really, absolutely no reason to expect a pedestrian stagger-ing along a lonely highway, sweat streaming down his face. At least I could hear the cars approaching from a good distance. So I'd drift off the shoulderless road into the waist high grass, reemerging when the vehicle was safely past. Each time I reemerged onto the smooth sur-face, my blue jeans were black with ticks. Just as I got them all wiped away, my shoulders would sag with the sound of another approaching vehicle that would start the whole process over again. This went on for at least, a couple of hours, as my pace slowed and my mouth dried to cotton. As was typical, I had no water with me, dehydration not having yet been invented for those of us living distant from the desert. Eventually, I dragged my sorry self in, removing seventy-six ticks from my clothes and person.

After dinner, my parents headed down the hill to visit with my grandparents. I declined the invitation to tag along, having had plen-ty of activity for one day. But as the Sun dropped, the air cooled and my cells were rehydrated, the lure of casting for bass was too strong to resist, and I headed to the shallow upper end of my uncle's pond. With the full Moon rising, I spied the wake of a large bass vacuuming up nesting bluegill. My gold topwater minnow landed gently two feet in front of the V. After a brief pause, one crank was all it took for the bass to crush the lure, an eventful close to an eventful day.

On a gray December day nearly two months after flushing a Wis-consin woodcock, we were hunting Grandpa Place on the property of my mother's youth, looking for grouse, but the grouse were already as good as gone in Indiana. As we walked a field road to get to a new section of forest, my childhood friend was cracking peanuts out of the shell, popping them into his mouth, my dad flanking him on the left and I on the right. On a lark, I turned into a short-grass cutout where my uncle's family camped, in case a covey of bobwhite quail was present. It was a lark because we hadn't seen quail on the property in years. They were struggling everywhere, the long tradition of southern bobwhite hunting disappearing rapidly. I can still picture peanuts flying, as a covey erupted from thin grass ten yards in front of me and flew right at my companions. Otherwise disposed, my friend had no chance to get a shot, but Dad got his first quail in maybe twenty or more years. I watched parts of the covey bank back through the woods, a few singles dropping into the tall grass of the gas pipeline that transected the property. We angled out onto the pipeline, and I put up one of the singles at my feet, knocking it down as it circled back toward the woods. It was the only time my dad and I ever took quail on the same day.

We were ebullient as we strode back to the truck, laughing and talking while covering the ground where my mother had milked cows and slaughtered chickens for Sunday dinners, where I learned to fish and hunt and love the land. Maybe the quail were coming back after all, and it would be a long future of wood ducks covering the streams, pheasants for every holiday meal, grouse in every northeast Iowa woodland, and quail back where quail belonged. It seems a little on the nose to point out that storm clouds were building directly behind us, literally. To the west, the sky had grown ominous, brooding, molten. That night it snowed and snowed. More than a foot of heavy, wet, killing snow fell, with a flooding spring to follow, a dreaded one-two punch for ground-nesting wild birds. Those were the last quail I have seen.

YEAR 4

Incongruity

If you have no history with woodcock hunting—participating in it, reading about it, or hearing tales from those who do or did these things—then it is likely you know little about where they are found and how they are hunted, woodcock not even managing to be misunderstood as mythical creatures the way snipe are. Woodcock thrive in thick second-growth forest, areas with a dense understory of shrubs, often in wet bottomlands but with larger trees somewhere nearby. The understory might be so dense as to seem nearly impenetrable at times. Somewhere along the line, as the trips around the Sun keep piling up, the places woodcock hang out get more impenetrable for me with each arriving autumn. If you do know woodcock hunting, then it is very likely that ruffed grouse and ruffed grouse hunting are what you most closely associate with woodcock, both species often hanging out in young clear-cuts of aspen or "popple." To these folks it might seem odd, out of place, maybe even disconcerting that I most associate wood ducks with woodcock and woodcock hunting.

My parents always timed their fall visit to Iowa to stretch across the start of pheasant season, which also happened to be the peak of woodcock migration and when many wood ducks were still around. My teaching schedule usually allowed me to protect Thursday morning for an early hunt before venturing in to work. I could also manage the occasional late afternoon, when we would squeeze in an hour of hunting.

In the year following our birdless Wisconsin adventure, it had already been another interesting season of hunting before my parents arrived. It was the year I discovered snipe, learning instantly to recognize the distinctive bark of the "scaip" sound they make when they launch into the air. I had bagged three and missed more than that. Not only were they little wizards on the wing, but they nearly always flushed when one leg was hopelessly mired while the other leg was merely almost hopelessly mired. It was the first of thirteen consecutive years when I would bag at least one snipe. If woodcock hold the top spot in my heart and imagination, snipe are not far behind. On the surface they appear similar to woodcock, long bill built for probing for dinner, similar coloring and size, although snipe strike me as much more svelte, and they have interesting orange on the tail, where woodcock sport stark black and white. One of the things I appreciate about snipe on the wing, in the hand, or on the plate is the knowledge that so many people know them as mythological creatures, like bigfoot, chupacabra, or yeti. Never mind the prominent role they played in early Russian literature. Reading a little of a passage of Leo Tolstoy's *Anna Karenina*, translated by Joel Carmichael in the 1981 Bantam edition—"But just then both suddenly heard a piercing whistle that seemed to flick them by the ear; they both seized their guns, there were two flashes of lightning, and two shots rang out at the same moment. The high-flying snipe folded its wings instantly and fell into the thicket, bending down the slender young shoots"—before heading to the marsh to find snipe of my own is a favorite activity that connects me to a larger world. While dense cover can make woodcock shooting tricky, I find snipe shooting far more challenging, despite the lack of cover once the birds clear the marsh grass. They zig when I expect a zag. They get to top speed quickly, and with my feet mired at different levels, twisting to follow their erratic departure is an awkward, wrenching affair, not the poetic, graceful form an Olympic shooter displays while sporting a smile unspattered by marsh muck and slime.

In the preface to his 2020 *With Wings Extended: A Leap into the Wood Duck's World*, Greg Hoch writes, "it's easy to manage for woodcock and golden-winged warblers. It may be more challenging, however,

to manage for woodcock and wood ducks on the same parcel." This challenge makes sense. Wood ducks and woodcock require trees at opposite ends of their lifespans, the ducks needing very old trees with cavities for nesting and the upland birds requiring new growth forest. But I quickly learned that Iowa trout streams were one of the places the two could thrive together. I not only found birds there in fall hunting seasons but saw evidence of mating activity, in the form of woodcock sky dancing and wood ducks with broods trailing, during spring and early summer.

The Department of Natural Resources actively managed this coexistence in some places by making clear-cuts near streams, but the best locales, the ones that have produced both woodcock and wood ducks year after year are naturally occurring. I am not the first to notice this. In his 1997 book, *Timberdoodle Tales*, Tom F. Waters has an entire chapter devoted to finding woodcock along trout streams. A collision of the wildly disparate realities of my history, my inclinations, and natural history led to the wood duck and the woodcock becoming inextricably intertwined in my outdoor existence.

It was the Thursday before the pheasant opener, and I had arranged things so I could do an early morning hunt with my dad before work. The plan was to arrive early at Arroyo Place. We would be at the first hole on the trout stream just after legal shooting for ducks had started—a half hour before sunrise. From there, we would jump all the holes to the back of the property, a practice that requires knowing where the birds are most likely to be loafing on the stream, staying well away from the water before turning at a right angle to crash toward water's edge. Sometimes it works. When it does, I always figure it was less about my being stealthy and more about the birds deducing that surely something so clumsy couldn't be stalking them. After this effort, we'd return to the truck to change gear and head back in for a grouse and woodcock hunt shortly after it was legal shooting for those species.

Most of our jump shooting for the day was done, without us seeing a bird, when we hatched a plan for the very back hole. My dad would circle through the woods to the calm pool. With any luck he'd raise a bird or two and get a shot. I'd stay back downstream by a straight run of flowing water we know as "the good bank" when we are trout fishing. If my dad raised ducks, one just might choose to knife through the trees following the watercourse downstream right past me. It wasn't exactly rocket science, but it was a decent plan to engage two people in an activity more suited to a lone hunter.

As my dad started his stalk to the final hole, I eased up to the water's edge to wait. Hard to say who was more startled, me or the wood duck that burst out from the bank beside me. I'm going to go with me, because clearly the duck had been sitting there no more than fifteen feet away, listening to us discuss our plan. Being the cool and collected suave hunter that I am, I did what wouldn't be a stretch to call "panic." I wish I could say that it was somehow out of character and completely unexpected. I threw the gun to my shoulder and fired way, way, way too fast. In those days I hunted with a 12-gauge Remington 870, and I was pretty quick on the pump that ejected the empty and chambered a live shell. I took my second shot when the bird was still closer than was ideal but a little nearer to where it should have been had I waited and breathed before taking the first shot. The second shot plopped the duck into the weeds at stream's edge. As I hurried up to where it fell, the duck jumped out into the flow, headed downstream in a hurry. Without a dog, I always try to get to downed birds quickly, before any that are wounded have a chance to gather their wits. It's also a good idea to reload. I had not. At least I had one shot left, but I needed to let the bird get out a bit before taking that shot. The trouble was that if it got out too far it would disappear around a corner in the current. Somehow, I managed it perfectly and dispatched the bird such that it drifted into an eddy for an easy retrieve. Like I said, never any panic.

Now, if you count yourself among those who knew woodcock hunting sufficiently to be surprised by my connecting wood ducks and woodcock, then likely you are near dismay at my hunting either species without a dog. A reader might even be downright suspicious that I lack the capacity for reason, given my willingness to admit this failure in print. Fair enough. Many of our most troubling character flaws must have components that are traceable to roots developed during our formative years. My approach to hunting is surely no exception. Since we never hunted with a dog, I grew up without knowledge that some people might share time afield with canine companionship. We had no animals in or around the house. My parents had a photo—it was a slide, for anyone who recalls such things—that showed my recently married mother holding freshly skinned squirrels ready for the dinner pot. She hated that image. Having grown up milking cows and butchering chickens, for her it was a sign that she had made it when she could leave all that behind, delighted to never have another animal near. There was no way we would have had a hunting dog. Still, some were around. I knew Dan the Brittany and Charlie the German shorthair (as well as my favorite, Dudley the basset hound) at my dad's parents. Why we didn't hunt with these dogs, I've no idea. Perhaps they hunted with someone but not that I knew of.

By the time I was settled in Iowa, I certainly had the opportunity to correct this shortcoming, but the busyness of that niche job that landed me in this special place made the thought of doing right by a dog daunting in those early days. It wouldn't have been fair to the dog. Imagine it like buying a blank canvas and slopping paint on it. Sure, there are plenty of canvases in the world, but I would always look at that canvas and ache a little, knowing what it might have been in different hands. My lack of specialization—roaming miles per day looking for half a dozen different species of birds—wasn't a hunting style designed perfectly for a dog either.

To be thorough with this analysis, I must confess that I also have been, to some degree, wary of the relationship I would develop with a hunting dog. I have developed remarkably special bonds with the dogs that have graced my adult life, singing to them regularly. I recall TV fishing host Jerry McKinnis once saying something like, "Without a dog who would I sing to?" and Kristin noting the accuracy of the sign in the vet's office that said, "After the dog, honey, you're number one." These quotations pretty much nail it. Dogs are also great to joke with, and that reminds me of a patio umbrella story. I deemed this device perfectly fine despite a broken crank that required the user to put his head up under the closed umbrella to push it open. These days, I am much more cautious about cavalierly thrusting my head into dark, narrow caves. Call it the wisdom of maturity. One fateful day, before the wisdom of maturity, as I reached to push the umbrella open, I thought, "Huh, that's odd. A small clump of leaves just fell on my shoulder." The whole incident lasted a second or two as the clump of leaves sprang to life, dancing all over my head and shoulders, both of us trying to find the nearest exit from the umbrella cave where the bat had been peacefully minding its own business before some bear aggressively attacked it. Did the bat bite me? I don't know. Did the bat scratch me? I don't know, despite scratches all around my neck and shoulder. I live the kind of existence where scratches aren't exactly rare. Bats being the number one cause of human rabies cases in the United States, my physician called the state veterinarian for Iowa, that being the official procedure for any potential human rabies contact. I teased the dog, reminding her that she only had an ordinary vet. I got treatment advice from the *state* vet. My personal vet, the state vet, said, "Of course he should get rabies shots. Better safe than dead."

No doubt that all this canine love would be amped up further with a hunting dog. Much ink has been spilled about the importance of the relationship between human and canine hunters, with some writers proclaiming that without the magic of that relationship they would forgo hunting; the hunt is for the dogs and dog work in the field is of utmost importance. Given my special bond with dogs, it's not hard to imagine my going down that path to the point that it eventually drove me away from hunting. If something about a day afield rises to be more important than recognizing that a living, breathing animal is losing its life, then for me, it's time to reconsider the point of the whole business. Hunter, landscape, and bird must maintain a balance but with the role of the bird remaining central.

My philosophizing about the nature of the relationship between hunter and bird or hunter and landscape may sound like preaching or even complaining about how others go about their craft. Of course, that may be part of it, since very little in life is entirely one thing or another, but I certainly don't begrudge bird hunters their experience when dogs represent the core of that experience. I trust they don't begrudge me my approach, wary of anything that might supplant the bird at the apex of the activity. An approach is less about being right or wrong and more about being true to both oneself and the world. Despite time running out, I still expect dogs will one day be part of my bird hunting. For years, I subscribed to *Pointing Dog Journal* and even had a breeder of French Brittanys I was keeping an eye on.

Hunting without dogs and linking wood ducks and woodcock aren't the only places where seemingly inconsistent realities coexist. Some might even think my dual obsession with outdoor pursuits and astrophysics falls in that realm. Certainly, what we know as wave-particle duality does. Einstein's Nobel prize came from his work on understanding how light interacts with metals to kick out electrons, the photoelectric effect mentioned in chapter Year 1. This interaction can only be understood if light behaves as a collection of particles, like a stream of tennis balls, a single electron firing out of the metal in a predictable way, with predictable speed every time a photon of light lands a direct hit on the electron in the metal, as particle (photon) strikes particle (electron). Except we already knew light was not a stream of particles but a wave with its energy distributed in space like the energy of ripples on a pond, spread out over an area, not localized in one spot like the energy of a tennis ball. That distributed energy is utterly unable to suddenly eject an electron at high speed. The experiments that showed light was definitely a wave were done a century before Einstein's groundbreaking work. Light isn't a bunch of particles waving around, up and down. That reality wouldn't produce the experimental results that show light as waves. You do one experiment, and you get light to look like thing A. You do another experiment, and you get light to look like thing B. If we try to construct a simple mental image of what light is, we struggle because in our image light can't be both A and B. When light behaves as particles, those particles are quanta, the single smallest unit something can have. In the United States, the quantum of money is the cent. We can claim something to be a fraction of a cent as we do with gasoline, but when it is time to settle up, we can't pay a fraction of a cent. The study of quanta grew into what people call quantum mechanics, a thoroughly successful model of the world that rests on two things that our brains can't quite seem to make fit together.

Back on the day that wood ducks and woodcock became strongly linked for me, my father and I deposited the wood duck in the truck and headed back out, just as planned. We would cross the stream above a very large and deep hole (we refer to it as the "front hole" because it is at the very front of the property; poets we are) that is popular among anglers who sit in lawn chairs and drift corn to trout. Things have changed so much over the years that we might have a hard time pulling off this hunt now, the area having become such a tourist destination that anglers are always around it seems. Maybe early on a cool October weekday morning it would still work. Maybe. Across from this hole is a flat floodplain filled with brush and small trees, the heavy cover continuing on up the bluff beyond. It is all picture postcard beautiful, making it little wonder the area has become so popular.

At the riffles where we intended to cross, I gently placed my 870 on the bank beside me and knelt to wash duck blood from my hands. As I did so, a woodcock flushed from my left and flew across the stream, landing just a few yards onto the floodplain. I thought I had marked the bird down pretty well and lined my dad up for where I expected the reflush. I always wanted to get my father into birds, but knowing how important woodcock are to me each fall, I might not be so magnanimous now. Or maybe I wasn't then. I just thought I was. You see, the bird's next flush was directly in front of me. The bird disappeared briefly behind a small cedar before popping into the clear for an open shot that I managed. We hunted an hour or so more without seeing anything else, and I made it to work by 10:30 with two very fine birds resting in the fridge. Two days later, my mother's sister passed away and our annual hunting together was cut short for other important things.

YEAR 5

Evolving Aims

Although it was a bit of a hit-or-miss affair, I was settling into my
role as a woodcock hunter in a new land just as I was settling into my
role as an astronomer at a small school focused more on preparing
students to excel in the world beyond than on generating knowledge
of the universe for the sake of knowledge of the universe. The year
that followed my first woodcock–wood duck double was the second
year in three that I failed to bag a woodcock. That hasn't happened
since, and it serves as evidence of the not yet smoothly rolling forward
nature of my woodcock hunting.

My only woodcock encounter this year came while a friend and I
were hunting the woods by a river, one regularly referred to as Iowa's
most scenic. It's crawling with kayakers these days; less so then. While
I have wandered these hills gun in hand occasionally, the property is
not part of my regular hunting rotation, although it is near the top of
preferred fishing properties. Kristin and I do hike-in angling here, the
water being a top producer of walleye, sauger, trout, and smallmouth
bass, while being sufficiently close to the Mississippi that all sorts of
other fish are possible, including white bass, which are more likely
to show up in our catch here than at any of our other regular angling
venues. One year, where a cornfield abuts mature oak forest, very near
a favorite fishing hole, we walked up on a freshly eviscerated young
fawn with a gut pile built neatly to its side, not an everyday Iowa sight.
You know, "That must've been one tough, mean cow." Near the spot of
the eviscerated fawn, we once nearly stepped on a mature rattlesnake,
the only one I have encountered in Iowa. Another time, on the drive to

this property, we had to brake to a stop as two gray partridge, known as Hungarian partridge or "huns" to hunters, attempted to corral an amazing swarm, twenty-two I believe, of tiny, tiny chicks across the road. The chicks buzzed around like bumble bees. They'd be almost across the road when two would peel off back toward the centerline and one of the bedraggled adults would give chase as another one or two chicks leaked out of the swarm in a different direction. I've read that Hungarian partridge are very short-lived, and I can see why. Just getting that brood safely across the road one time must've have taken months if not years off their parents' lives. Where the river makes a hard right bend, the terrain is such that the water misses that turn and barrels straight ahead during major flood events. On three separate occasions following particularly robust floods, three different refrigerators have been deposited at nearly the exact same spot on this bend, leading me to mangle a line of poetry from Robert Frost into "Something there is that loves a fridge that wants it there." We'll refer to this beautiful property as Refrigerator Bend Place.

This year a friend and I were kicking around the property looking for rabbits, as he is an avid hunter of cottontails. At one point in the hunt, we both looked up at a passing lone Canada goose with another, apparently smaller bird above it. Except the "smaller" bird kept getting bigger and bigger until it was clear that it was the larger bird, and it was diving hard on the goose that was flying with all it had. The bald eagle, about as abundant as blue jays around here these days, slammed the goose in midair, both of them tumbling from sight behind a nearby hill. In our collective decades of living outdoors, neither of us had ever seen anything quite like that, a bird of that immensity hawking another huge bird out of midair. This had been no kestrel on sparrow attack or even owl on woodcock. We continued back in silence, mulling over the scene.

As the end of a long, fruitless hunt neared, the river lay on our left, with a dense but exceedingly narrow strip of woods between us and the flow. A field planted in, of all things, flowers was on our right. I've no idea who was farming those flowers or why, but they were sufficiently sparse that they gave the field a barren feel, nearly empty compared to the typical corn or soybean fields around. Despite my fatigue, I opted to walk the narrow strip of cover, hoping to kick a rabbit out in front of my friend. Saying I was unprepared when the woodcock flushed and flew thirty yards straight away is a bit like saying the snakes I stepped on barefoot as a youngster aroused some interest in me. Still, I managed to react sufficiently to miss a shot. On the reflush, bizarrely, the bird flew out into the flower field. I missed again. We combed that field, carefully searching where the woodcock had landed but saw no hint of the bird, despite the openness of the land. That's how well their feathering hides them. Still a bird sitting on bare ground simply had to be visible. After a minute or two of close inspection, we turned to leave, and the woodcock flushed behind us, precisely where we had been searching. As it flew out over the open field, we both missed. It was time to go home.

As I had been growing familiar with all these places to hunt and fish and learning to hunt new birds, I had pivoted to an entirely new research project. The detectors we had been developing in California utilized ultraviolet light emission from xenon gas when struck by an X-ray or gamma-ray. Physicists refer to this emission as "scintillation," much to the chagrin of astronomers for whom the term refers to the buffeting of starlight coming through the atmosphere. Nothing can ever be simple. In Iowa, my teaching load was pretty heavy, leaving limited time for research, and eventually it felt like all my time in the lab that was intended to be used to learn more about xenon scintillation was instead devoted to repairing vacuum pumps and chasing leaks in the gas handling system. While the work was extremely valuable for students, the learning curve was steep, and high-pressure gas is dangerous—a caged tiger, a training film once called it. On top of all that (and more), I had dark skies above calling me. So I left the high energy astrophysics world of X-rays and gamma-rays behind and learned what I could about visible-light astrophysics. Reinventing myself as a stellar astrophysicist, I began taking images of the same small patch of sky (picture a quarter of your fingernail held at arm's length) every clear night from late February through early October, eventually amassing hundreds of millions of individual stellar brightness measurements, waiting patiently for a data mound sufficient to allow subtle changes over the decades to become noticeable. This work takes place with a telescope and camera mounted atop one of the college's science buildings, the equipment protected by a rolling roof, all provided by the first grant I received when I arrived at my new job.

Although the skies are dark, the atmosphere is damp and roiling, and the equipment is nothing compared to what one finds on mountain tops. We decided to take advantage of our access to the sky every clear night, measuring the brightness of more than 1,600 stars hundreds of times each night for decades. With such coverage on different timescales, we can overcome some of the limitations of the equipment and the site to find interesting phenomena that might be missed if we sampled the region once a year or once a decade. To make the most of this small advantage, it seemed important to ensure that we got data every night that the sky was clear enough to allow it, measuring and measuring and measuring. I planned trips around nights when the Moon was too full and too near our study area to allow observation. I've often wondered if this is how dairy farmers feel, knowing that the cows needed milking every day, just as the telescope and camera need to acquire data every clear day for me. Thomas Edison is often credited with the observation, "Genius is one percent inspiration and 99 percent perspiration." I'm not sure about genius, but the quotation does capture an important truth regarding how progress gets made, whether it be in looking for subtle changes in the stars or getting better at hunting woodcock. Also important is the recognition that outcomes are nearly always made of multiple inputs. When describing some problem facing society, too often you hear people say, well, X isn't the problem or X is the problem—you know, overpopulation isn't the problem, guns aren't the problem, high taxes aren't the problem, eating too much sugar isn't the problem—as if multiple things can't contribute to an issue. To explore this idea more fully, let's use the language of linear combinations. An example of a linear combination of x, y, and z might be $ax + by + cz$, where a is the weighting of input x, b is the weighting of input y, and c is the weighting of input z. If we normalize things so that $a + b + c = 1$, then these weights provide the fractional contribution of x, y, and z to the result. There can be any number of inputs. In Edison's genius example there were two inputs: inspiration and perspiration, and the weighting looks like $0.01 \times$ inspiration $+ 0.99 \times$ perspiration $=$ genius. Of course, there could be many inputs to genius instead of just two, like timing, luck, fortunate background, and more. It's a framework that reminds us that life is rarely as simple as "single cause" = "single effect" and helps us think about the relative importance of different inputs.

The most important part of my new research program was that it offered students the chance to work on a vast array of projects, projects rich in statistics and computer coding, leading to the chance for immense growth. Although the xenon gas research work had offered students tremendous opportunities to learn, the star data offered more of those opportunities to a bigger group of students. One of the first students who worked on the xenon project for a couple of years wrote a detailed and elegant senior thesis on the topic. When this student applied to graduate school, a faculty member from that institution called me and asked, "This student didn't really write this paper did he? It's too technical and too advanced." I assured my inquisitor that the student in question had, indeed, written the thesis and had developed remarkably as a scientist during the four years I knew him. When one of the first students to work on the new project applied to graduate school, a faculty member from that school called and asked, "She's not really as good as you say she is, is she? I come from a small liberal arts school so I know students might not be that prepared." When I assured this inquisitor that she was, indeed, that good and had grown remarkably as a scientist in the four years I knew her, he proceeded to try to break me down like a police interrogator. I am guessing that the amount of struggle I had in convincing these admission committee members of the great work these students were capable of was some linear combination of student gender identity, my level of eloquence, committee member experience, and probably many other things.

In the midst of multiple conversions—from high energy astrophysicist to visible light astrophysicist, from primarily researcher to primarily teacher, and from grouse and quail hunter to woodcock and wood duck hunter—my most memorable bird of this year came while I was jump-shooting the creek at Old Homestead Place at first light. I'd found no ducks, and the best holes were behind me, with but one or two remaining as the creek tumbled along on my right, an open field on my left, mature trees behind and ahead, and a limestone bluff climbing steeply away from the far bank of the stream. Twenty yards before me lay a flat plain parallel to but two feet below the one I was on. My adrenaline surged when I deduced that the lower plain was filling up with turkeys crossing the creek from the steep bluff. In stalk mode, I took six or eight minutes to cover twenty yards, hunching lower and lower as I went, the standard turkey cacophony issuing from ahead assuring me that the birds were going about their morning routine unaware of—or unconcerned with—my presence.

At the lip separating upper plain from lower plain, I straightened slightly to spy fifteen turkeys milling about the open forest, moving this way and that, the hubbub transforming the fifteen into a sea that was more of a single spreading turkey entity. Having sensed potential trouble, one head popped up, offering a clear shot. My trouble was that this bird and all the others were at least thirty-five yards out—maybe it was at least forty—and I was shooting #4 steel shot through an improved cylinder choke. Killing a turkey reliably, not leaving it wounded in the forest, requires pellets that hit hard in a tight circle centered on the bird's head since the feathers on the body are like armor that causes shotgun pellets to bounce off. Being less dense than other options, steel shot loses energy relatively quickly, making it less lethal at the distance of these birds. The improved cylinder choke allows the shot pellets to spread more quickly than they would with a tighter modified or much tighter full choke, meaning fewer pellets in the small circle centered on the turkey's head. No grizzled old veteran turkey hunter arising hours before the Sun to make a plan for the morning says, "I think I'll go with steel shot and an open choke." In planning a hunt, there is ample time to think about where to go and how to approach the cover, but when the critical shoot or don't shoot moment arrives, it is just that, a moment. Decide and live with it. Life always provides plenty of time for second guessing. That neck was not going to stay elongated while I calculated probabilities and decided, actuarially, where the threshold of acceptable risk lay. I squeezed the trigger and the big bird dropped without so much as a flap, while other confused turkeys scrambled, some circling closer to me, offering an excellent opportunity had I already possessed my second allowable turkey tag. For the remainder of that fall, until snow blanketed the land, I would go well out my way to walk past the pile of turkey feathers left there and recall that scene. To this day, the memory of that morning floods back whenever Kristin and I are trout fishing the idyllic stretch of water flowing nearby.

That turkey was memorable for another reason, it being the only bird I have shot and eaten as an adult that I didn't cook myself. The opportunity to share it with my parents when they arrived was a significant pleasure. Never mind that I had been cooking my own meals for more than twenty years; it would have been an affront to suggest to my mother that I, not she, roast that bird. It was an important signpost on the road of life when Kristin and I visited my parents, or especially when it was just me, and my mom no longer resisted, even slightly, if one or both of us cooked dinner. That long-ago turkey dinner is another thing that my father still comments on every now and then, usually prompted by my recounting a hunting story during our phone calls. "That was a delicious bird," he'll say, and he is right. It was a particularly delicious bird.

Information Densely Packed

By now, I was growing comfortable in my new home, the classroom, and the forests and fields, that newfound comfort leading, as it often does, to something of an itch to explore novel things, new species of birds or new spaces or hunting or teaching techniques. I shot two turkeys this time around and a goose of all things, a more or less once-in-a-decade occurrence. Standing corn served as my blind, with a dozen silhouette decoys, flat images of geese, spread across the grass separating the corn from a trout stream just above where it dumped into the river. Sporadically, as mosquitoes formed a writhing sphere around my head, a distant goose honked somewhere along the river, and I'd sound my call, utilizing all the skill and subtlety seventeen minutes of practice spread over three years yields. My mind had drifted. Maybe I was wondering whether the developer of mosquito repellant ever received a well-earned Nobel Prize, when I was jolted to attention, realizing that a group of geese somewhere out of sight had reacted to my feeble calling and was headed my way. For better or worse, I hit the call again, an action that, unfathomably, didn't deter them noticeably. The goose babble grew louder and louder until suddenly they were there, a squadron appearing over the trees ahead, wings set, intent on landing right on top of me, presumably looking to give honking lessons to the goose that had been annoying every other goose in the county all morning. That array of gray, black, and white behemoths coming in low is something to behold for one who dreams of diminutive woodcock and snipe. Momentarily rattled, I still managed to pick a bird and made the shot. The goose simply stopped flapping its wings, descending like a glider, thudding into the earth belly down and skidding to a stop, dead in the corn, looking for all the world like a plane that had managed a controlled landing following a landing gear failure. As is often the case when I succeed at something I rarely do, I thought, "I should do this more often," perhaps procuring an annual Christmas goose. But I ask you, where would that time come from? Life is about choices, made consciously or otherwise.

For the first time, I bagged two woodcock. My first woodcock encounter of the year occurred at Spring Fish Place. Excellent woodcock cover lined both sides of the road, and I spent a warm afternoon working through it. It is, by the way, the tickiest property I hunt, and on an early season outing such as this, it's possible for me to miss every bird flush while engaged in picking ticks off my pants. One side of the road is all bluff, with dense cover stretching nearly two-thirds of the way to the top from the gravel edge. Public land spreads out on top as well, and once I heard a rooster pheasant crowing up there. My most productive pheasant hunting occurs where I must climb through a difficult stretch of dense woods to get to open fields far from the parking area, so I stored this info for future use. But now the Department of Natural Resources (DNR) has gone and put a parking lot up top as well, dashing that plan before it reached fruition. This bluff side had been the more productive for grouse and I would, in time, flush woodcock here too. The opposite side of the road held flat bottomland covering a hundred-yard strip by the road before it too became bluff. In the flat bottomland, a dry creek bed paralleled the dusty road several feet below it.

I started my hunt on the bluff side, where I typically worked across the hill at one elevation until the dense cover emptied into a heart-meltingly beautiful little stretch of flat ground that simply had to hold birds but never did. Then I would change elevations and work back. On this day, I only hunted one direction before dropping down to cross the road to work the cover on the far side.

I traversed the dry creek near the road all the way to the river's edge before moving halfway across the flat and pushing back. When the good cover ran out, I turned 180 degrees once more for a last walk through cover, back toward the truck. By now I was weaving in and out of blowdowns where the flat plain rolled vertically into the bluff. Sometimes I was walking level terrain, and sometimes I was on the steep hillside. Nearly all the way back to the river, two woodcock came out of a single brush pile, arcing across the flat land toward the road. I dropped one bird as the other landed in dense berry briars near the dry creek bed. It was the earliest I'd ever bagged a woodcock, just over a week into the season. Following up on the bird in the briars, I was pretty sure I didn't really want a second bird from this property or a second bird this early in the season. When I stopped short of committing to the thorns, the woodcock came out, except once again it was a pair. As one crossed the road, and the other flew down the creek bed to my right. I watched them go before heading back to the truck, woodcock in game bag, wiping ticks from my pants.

Despite knowing the place's popularity with paddlers, I was startled when I got back to the truck and looked up from tick brushing to find a group of kayakers milling around where I was parked. They had taken out at the bridge, trying to determine what to do in the absence of the ride they were expecting. Not everybody is elated to see a hunter pop out of the woods, especially one maniacally wiping at his brush pants, but if they were concerned, they managed to conceal it, and one of them was sufficiently brave to hop in the truck with me for a ride back to their put-in vehicle. I hope he thought to check for ticks after disembarking my truck.

Like many of my favorite wild places, Spring Fish Place is a multi-use property for Kristin and me. We hike an old logging road up the hill and back down again, dropping in along the river to fish a stretch that's never the most productive water, although we always find a few walleye, smallmouth bass, and sauger. We also catch more odd rough fish here than anywhere else. There's a distinct pleasure in setting the hook and having no idea what might be on the other end, including buffalo, drum, mooneye, and carp in addition to the more common game fish. One cold, gray March day before the river had warmed sufficiently to warrant genuine hope of angling success, we reveled, nonetheless, in having turned the corner from snowy winter to a season of river and lake fishing. I was absent-mindedly retrieving a crankbait at molasses running speed when a fat-bellied perch hammered the offering, the only perch we have ever seen in any river around here. We catch some perch in our lakes, but they aren't the famous fish of the upper Midwest, ours being scrawny little things. This river perch, however, was closer to what folks where we go in Wisconsin might refer to as a teeter-pig, a chunk of a thing. Where did that perch come from? Had it run up the many miles from the Mississippi? Why have we never seen another one here in decades of angling? What was it doing hitting a crankbait in water that cold? Such are the mysteries that keep life interesting.

An echo of the joy of casting into a river with a realistic expectation that just about anything could strike can be found in the sky-monitoring project I started, where a star could flare unexpectedly for any number of reasons or asteroids could wander by or who knows what might happen just once. Compared to these rough fishlike one-offs, long-period pulsating variable stars (LPVs) and eclipsing binary star systems (EBs) are the smallmouth bass and walleye-like stars we can count on showing us something interesting with regularity.

The Sun is in a stage of existence where, deep in its innermost core, it is relatively quietly converting hydrogen, the lightest chemical element in the universe, into helium, the second lightest chemical element, through nuclear fusion. Consider a campfire that gives off energy that we see as a glow and feel as warmth. If there is no source of fuel then the fire dies away, the glow and warmth disappearing. Thus, we must continue providing logs for the fire to burn. If the energy input from the burning logs is equal to the energy being carried away as warmth and glow, then the fire continues, unchanging, in what we call a steady state or equilibrium. When nuclear fusion produces helium from hydrogen in the core, energy is produced, a lot more energy than one gets from campfire logs. As long as that energy is equal to the energy being radiated into space (the glow and warmth we get from the Sun, for example), the star continues emitting energy in a steady state. The high temperature associated with nuclear fusion yields a pressure from both matter and light. The "light" deep inside the Sun is better thought of as electromagnetic radiation in the form of X-rays and gamma rays. That pressure pushing outward works against gravity trying to collapse the star inward. Stars will naturally settle into a temperature and radius at which outward pressure perfectly balances inward pressure, creating a steady state equilibrium in which the star is neither shrinking nor growing. The Sun will be in this state of equilibrium (although the temperature and radius will change very, very gradually over time, so that it is really quasi-equilibrium) for about ten billion years, a lifetime it is more or less halfway through.

When the star runs out of hydrogen fuel in the core, the quasi-equilibrium must come to a jarring end, just as the quasi-equilibrium of anyone's life will be repeatedly disrupted by things far less predictable than the exhaustion of core hydrogen. When the energy input from nuclear fusion in the core ceases, the temperature in and around the core drops, resulting in a decrease in outward pressure that causes gravity to overcome the outward pressure and the inner layers of the star to contract. When things contract under the influence of an attractive force like gravity, they heat up. When they expand, they cool. This heating of the inner layers causes nuclear fusion to ignite in a thin shell around the core, and the star is now a red giant. Helium produced by this shell falls in toward the core until the core gets hot enough for the helium there to begin fusing into carbon. Quickly, in astronomical terms, the helium fusion ceases, the helium having become carbon, and

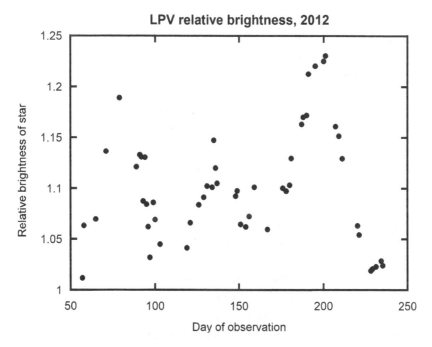

LPV relative brightness, 2012

the inner layers contract once more, leading to energy being produced in a hydrogen fusion shell and a helium fusion shell around the core. The star is now an asymptotic giant branch star. During parts of this phase of a star's life, maintaining equilibrium proves challenging, and the star pulsates, growing and shrinking, getting brighter and dimmer regularly. The more than seventy LPVs in the field we study are in this stage. The accompanying illustration is a brightness versus time graph (a light curve) for one of our stars.

The graph shows that the star is about 25 percent brighter at its brightest than it is at its faintest and that it takes about sixty-five days to go from brightest to faintest and back to brightest but that the star is at a different brightness level each time it reaches peak brightness—all mysteries we must explain if we wish to thoroughly model these stars. But we want to pause to admire the image itself; astronomers and physicists live and breathe graphs like this one because they contain so much information in a concise package. With a quick glance, I was able to see the key features of this star that needed modeling.

So attracted am I to this type of visualization that I graph data wherever I find data, and so attuned to understanding the world in terms of data am I that I find data everywhere. One of my absolute favorite graph types is a histogram. A histogram is like a bar chart but with a quantitative horizontal axis. The horizontal axis is a measure of something lumped into "bins." Think of the bins as a series of buckets; on the vertical axis we plot how many times our quantity of interest fell in the given bucket. For example, earlier I claimed that my first woodcock of the current year came earlier than in any previous year. If we want to make a histogram of when I have bagged woodcock, and of course I do, time is the quantity we will use on the horizontal axis. Two questions face us: (1) What do we use for the start of time and (2) how big should our buckets be? The answer to the first question doesn't matter too much as long as we remember what we choose. Let's call September 1 of any year Day 1. Then, for example, October 15 is Day 45, and November 1 is Day 62, and so on. The answer to the question of bucket size matters a great deal, and if you are a scientist looking for an interesting signal in your data, how you answer this question might determine whether or not you see that signal. If we choose a bucket size of one day, then all the birds I have bagged on October 20 over the years will be in the bin stretching from fifty to fifty-one (or 49.5 to 50.5 depending on how I have chosen to set up my bins). But since I have only shot twenty-three woodcock in twenty-two years, it's possible that very few birds have fallen on any one day and such a histogram might look like a patternless smattering of bars. I could make my bin size be fifty or one hundred days but then all my birds would fall in one or two bins, and again no pattern would emerge. All we can do is try different bin sizes to see what appears. As shown below, it turns out that choosing a bin size of one day works pretty well in this particular case.

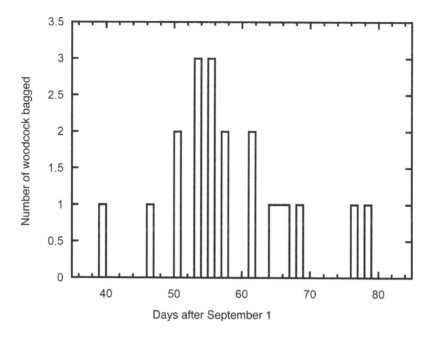

Just as with the LPV light curve, we get a quick insight into my woodcock hunting. The upper and lower limits (about Day 80 and Day 40 respectively) are largely set by regulations determining legal hunting seasons. There is a strong peak between about Days 50 and 62, the end of October. In fact, we learn that my most productive hunting times are the weekend just before Halloween and the college's fall break, which occurs a week to ten days earlier. We also see that I do find birds before and after those peak times. Long ago, I read an article suggesting that Iowa's woodcock seasons were too early, that birds were migrating through the state largely after our seasons ended. The author called for Iowa to shift woodcock season later in the year. Think back to our discussion of the process of science in chapter Year 2. What really makes science science is that a model makes a specific prediction that can be tested observationally. In this case, any model showing that Iowa woodcock seasons end too early would lead to a prediction that our histogram would have its bars shifted to the right edge of the graph, that most of my woodcock would have come near season's end. My data set is inconsistent with the proposed model, but we must be very careful to recognize that I am just one hunter, hunting in a particular way in a tiny part of the state. Before we completely reject the proposed model, more data would be needed. I confess that the primary purpose of these graphs is not usually model testing for me. I find my wife, a woodland stream, a starry night, and a woodcock to be about the most beautiful things in the world, but graphs of star or bird data are very close.

Let's also return to our concept of the linear combination and ask what fraction of my love of data and graphs is innate and what part has arisen as a result of my learning and my choice of profession? If it's a 50/50 split, we would write $0.50 \times$ innate $+ 0.50 \times$ learned. There is a bit of data that suggests it might be more innate than that. As a child, I built entire sports leagues from various sports games I had, creating teams full of players who had seasons of games against one another, primarily so that I could calculate the player stats and build league leader boards. Perhaps my affinity for poetry is also largely innate and related to my love of graphs, both poems and graphs building right to the essence of what is there, but with layer on layer to unfold with time and study. There's more to it than that. The essay and the full scientific paper are important for the details, the things you must know to make sure you have the story straight and to ensure a full record for those who come after. The poem and the graph envelop the essential part of the idea, but for me, their true value lies in the feelings they evoke. I feel more connected to the story when I see it visually in graphical form or hear it flowing in poetic form.

One beauty of the Spring Fish Place stretch of river, where I bagged my first woodcock of the year, lies in it being the first to come alive in the spring for us. Brown trout—and to a lesser extent rainbows that wash out of the stocked trout streams—take up residence there, where they get large, muscular, and feisty, altogether different entities from when they were dumped from the back of a truck. Don't get me wrong. We enjoy our share of fishing all trout streams but introduce utter novices to trout angling at both the stocked streams and Spring Fish Place and those beginners might doubt they were partaking of the same activity at each place. At Spring Fish Place, the hiking is hard; the water is fast; and the fish hit like locomotives. It all starts as soon as the snowmelt lets us in, lasting until late April or early May, when the trout more or less vanish as the bass and walleye grow aggressive. This spring transition is marked by one of the best wildflower progressions around. Dropping down the hill in March, we see our first trillium of the season. Two weeks later, all kinds of wildflowers erupt. One stretch of hill above the old road becomes a sea of Dutchman's breeches stretching out of sight. By the end of April, they have faded to sporadic clumps as bloodroot becomes dominant in the woods, along with plentiful anemone, bellwort, and spring beauty. When we think the show is over, the flowers having dried to a trickle from a torrent, suddenly phlox is everywhere before columbine and wild geranium signal the impending transition to a more muted summer. For five consecutive years, our best morel hunting occurred here as well, but that spot has aged out the same way a woodcock clear-cut will.

This spring eruption arrives at precisely the right time. I need the light, the color, and the new life, despite my being an autumn into winter person who appreciates chilly air, bird hunting, and shortening days. And I welcome the dark more than most. We are losing the night sky from above as satellite clusters now bombard astronomical images and from below as people want light flooded into every corner of existence, the dark brazenly banished from our lives. Certainly, I aggressively oppose light pollution for professional reasons, but also for human and personal reasons, the night sky having been not only critical for the development of what we know as science but equally as

a resource of wonder and inspiration for people for countless generations. The night sky reminds us of our oneness on this planet together
while nudging us to remember the greater, the larger, the beyond.
Alas, with limited recreational value and even more limited financial
value, the darkness and the heavens above are a resource difficult to
protect. Still, despite my love of darkness and the heavenly glimpse it
provides and despite my affection for the air of autumn and winter,
there comes a time when enough is enough. That time is somewhere
in February. Just in the nick of time, the transition back toward the
light becomes undeniably palpable, and even I, lover of the night and
cherisher of the cold, begin to dream of days at Spring Fish Place just
around the corner, and I feel the collective joy of humanity when it
can no longer be doubted that there is a light that the darkness has
not and shall not overcome.

My second woodcock of the year came from a property we can refer
to as Big River Place, seeing as it lies near the Mississippi. Like Old
Homestead Place, it covers thousands of acres and has multiple entry
points, some "up top" and at least one "down below." Down below,
where I was hunting with my dad about two weeks after bagging the
first woodcock of the year, there were a couple of isolated clear-cuts
along the main valley floor of the property. A few years earlier, my
dad and I had each shot a grouse out of one of them, breaking my rule
of never shooting more than one grouse from any property. But we
bend rules a little when it comes to family. I had shot the first grouse,
and with birds in the area, I didn't want to deny my dad his chance.

Around the hill that bordered this main valley on the north was
another clear-cut. This one ran along the gravel road that paralleled
the property. It spread across the hill, covering an area greater than the
other two cuts combined. The north hill cut was dense and beautiful
but aging out, unfortunately. It was, in fact, the last place in Iowa
I could count on seeing grouse. I was still flushing them when the
DNR recut it. I was conflicted. Given its age, that clear-cut wouldn't

provide needed cover for birds much longer. Cutting was a more than reasonable choice, but with all my other reliable grouse coverts dried up, I was about to lose ruffed grouse altogether.

As we circled into this forest, a grouse got up in front of Dad, and he missed a tough shot. We were not yet actually into the clear-cut proper but in the brushy edge that bordered its east end. As we headed in the general direction the grouse had flown, a woodcock launched up between us, twice as close to me as it was to my dad. I fired my first shot far too fast but recovered to make a proper second shot. At this point in our unfolding narrative, I have bagged five woodcock in six years, a span of time equivalent to about 0.0000006 percent of the time the Sun will spend in its quasi-equilibrium state, fusing hydrogen into helium in its core.

YEAR 7

Ups and Downs

The story of woodcock in my life is part of a larger story of my having taken game or fish every month for more than twenty-one years. I've kept that streak going largely by just doing what I do, although more than a couple of times, I have had to work pretty hard in the bitter cold to keep the streak alive. As much as anything, what the early days of the streak represented for me was maybe what people mean when they talk about balance in life, recognition of the need for something that kept me in touch with the land when enclosed spaces threatened to devour all my time. Over the years, the feel of the project has evolved into something more like a sense of my own personal equilibrium, a grounding, a rolling wheel, a continuity. Each year is like the year before it, though given the stochastic nature of reality, no two are identical. Every time a few hundred million things happen, a whole lot of them are bound to be "Well isn't that odd" one-in-a-million events, and there will be a whole heck of a lot of still pretty unexpected one-in-a-thousand events, ensuring no two days in the field or anywhere else can be the same, let alone any two years.

When you are way out on one of the "Well isn't that odd" tails, people tend to call it bad luck. Way out on the other tail is deemed good luck, and I suppose it is if you are using the word "luck" to mean the occurrence of something improbable, an acceptable definition. I consider it extremely good luck that when I was seeking a job in a terribly narrow slice of the employment world, I landed where I did, doing what I do, but truth be told, many outcomes of that job search could have led to me reflecting on my good fortune all these years later.

What I have learned over three plus decades of teaching physics ideas is that people have a strong bias against believing that such events are nothing more than random, chaotic happenstance, bad things just happening, good things just happening. Even Einstein struggled with this concept, claiming that no God would play dice with the universe, leaving important matters to random chance. He was referring not to the bad and good luck that follow each of us around, riding the tails of a Gaussian distribution, but to the concept in quantum mechanics that it is fundamentally impossible to know some things. When we do an experiment that measures the electron in an atom as a particle, we can claim the probability of finding that electron at some position, and that probability is independent of where we last measured the electron. Further, sometimes we find the electron at point A and then later at point B but there may be a point between A and B where the electron can never be found, meaning it did not move from A to B. There are simply probabilities of finding the electron at different positions, no moving around or predicting the future based on what we just measured. That randomness is what Einstein was decrying, just as people may decry any apparent randomness in life.

Perhaps the data describing my bird hunting success, like the data describing many apparent good and bad luck experiences, can be very roughly approximated by something called Poisson statistics, although Poisson statistics would never fully capture the results of things so complex. Here's how it works. I know. I know. There's no way you could have imagined the good fortune of a statistics lesson popping up in this story. You, my friend, are riding *way* out on the good luck tail of things. Soak it up. If something has a fixed probability of happening each time you try it, the resulting number of times that thing happens given a certain number of tries will conform to a distribution that we call Poisson. "What?" you say.

Let's assume for a moment that the six colors of M&Ms in a regular bag are all equally represented in the bag (party size, of course) you just bought. It is an unquestioned fact that the orange ones are the best, and you hope for a few every time you pull out a handful. You have a one-in-six chance of getting orange each time you grab a single candy. Thus, the most likely number of orange candies you would get in a handful of twelve, would be two—⅙ × 12. This result comes with a caveat. The color of the candy you draw next has to be independent of the color of any candies already drawn. This, however, is not strictly true. If your first eleven pulls are all orange, then there are fewer orange candies left to pull for the twelfth candy. But if the bag is big enough (and still pretty full) and the candies well mixed, then the expectation that one out of six candies will be orange each time might be a good enough approximation. That's what we have to ask ourselves when we do data analysis or build a model of the universe: "This model isn't exactly right, but is it good enough to help us understand how the system works as long as we always keep in mind the model's limitations?" And that's where trouble often arises, when we fall in love with a model and forget that it was an approximation with limitations.

Now we all know that when you grab twelve candies, sometimes you get zero and sometimes you get six or more orange candies. Let's count the times you get each number. Suppose you are at a party, and you pull twelve M&Ms from a really, really large bowl one thousand times. Good party. You can count the number of times you got zero, the number of times you got one, got two, got three, and so on up to twelve. The result is more or less a Poisson distribution of numbers—again assuming your eating the candy didn't noticeably change the distribution of colors in the bowl (perhaps it was refreshed after each handful) and neglecting the hard cutoff of twelve at the upper end. It's probably OK not to worry about that upper limit because our expected average number of two is so far below twelve that drawing anything close to twelve will be pretty uncommon. There is a mathematical formula that describes a Poisson distribution; it predicts the number of times you will get zero, one, two, etc. Most people would call this scatter in the number you pull "noise," and I am OK if you do, although noise usually refers to something different, and if you want to sound particularly impressive at your M&M party, you'll call the distribution of different numbers of orange candies pulled Poisson counting statistics or something similar. I have actually used this stuff as the backbone of a couple of different published papers related to the emission of scintillation light from xenon gas. You see, it's often difficult to tell exactly how much light you are detecting, but much easier to tell whether you did or did not detect light. You can dial down the light intensity to the point that sometimes you detect it and sometimes you don't. Dump energy into your xenon one thousand times, detect light six hundred times, and you have four hundred zeroes in your Poisson distribution. Use that number to calculate the mean of the distribution, using the aforementioned mathematical formula, and the result is a measurement of how much light was emitted. Nice, right?

Probably, one of the ways I differ from most people I meet is that I tend to think of more or less everything in terms of Poisson counting statistics or related probabilistic ideas, even going so far as badgering my father with it. He almost certainly thought I was taunting him, when really, I was trying to teach basic statistical thinking, an act much crueler than simple taunting. I can't help it. We would be fishing when the first two bass of the day would hit my lure. Even if we were doing everything identically, Poisson counting statistics tells us that there was a decent chance I might catch the first two fish on any day. But truth be told, I was more likely to catch those fish because I was more serious about fishing and fished more, meaning I was better at it, better at casting, better at reading the water and the weather, and so on, just because I did it so much more often. Plus, I was more intense on the water. My dad always loved fishing, but for him the term "fishing" was broadened to encompass watching the sunrise, stopping to eat a Bit-O-Honey, and maybe even dozing in the boat's pedestal chair. Thus, I might make fifteen casts for every ten he made, and they were frequently better—or at least gutsier—casts, closer to snags and trouble. Still, after I caught a couple of bass, he would often switch lures to what I was using. To be ornery, I'd switch to something else just to make the case that catching a few fish can't tell us exactly what is going on.

Now Poisson counting statistics only works if you have the exact same chance of getting the result you seek each time you do the trial, as I tried to emphasize by acting like we were refilling our bowl of M&Ms. Such an analysis will only ever be an approximation when predicting how many birds I bag each year because, for example, some years I hunt more diligently than others. Poisson counting statistics will never work at all for describing my annual woodcock take, because I tend to try pretty hard until I get that first bird, taking my foot off the accelerator thereafter. I am not "sampling" the woodcock in the same way each year, never mind all the other things that can vary. Think of it as if I were reaching into that M&M bag until I get my one, delightful orange disc, no matter how long it takes, then stopping or at least slowing way down.

In addition to the randomness that people might call noise but is maybe more like Poisson counting statistics, there is the slow, inevitable change that tracks everything. The world is always changing, however subtly. I am not the same hunter I was twenty years ago, and the landscape around me is not the same landscape, nor are bird populations the same. Doing the exact same bird sampling I did twenty years ago would be impossible, no matter how much I might ache to do so. The real value in thinking about this *like* Poisson counting statistics, though not *exactly* Poisson counting statistics, is that it provides a framework, a structure for us to use to picture the kind of randomness that sits atop everything else. I might hunt the exact same willow thicket in the exact same way day after day, seeing a few birds many days, but scads of birds when the wind has blown them in, and no birds when the wind has blown them out. But now we are introducing this Poisson-like randomness on top of that. A slight breeze might have blown woodcock in a way that they happened to see my thicket and landed, or it might have blown them the other way so that they saw a different thicket and landed there. Likewise, my walking through the thicket a few feet to the left or right might lead toward or away from any particular bird, resulting in a flush one day and no flush another day. The result is a slightly uncomfortable model: cause = 73 percent chance of effect 1; 18 percent chance of effect 2; 8 percent chance of effect 3; and 1 percent chance other, rather than the more concrete cause = effect.

One way to picture these variations might be to see short term oscillations, like a rapidly varying wave, but much more chaotic, riding atop much more slowly varying changes that may also be ups and downs but could just move in a single direction, up or down, instead of up and down, like wetlands or prairies or second-growth forests disappearing. When you have that image in your mind, you are probably picturing a single axis, consisting of one wave or trend with another smaller one on top, all full of noise. Reality is more like that happening in every aspect of life. So you need to now picture that single axis spun around a vertical axis such that there are waves headed out in all directions, with each direction representing a different facet of life, some closer to stable, some varying dramatically, some displaying ups and downs, some displaying monotonic trends, some with multiple timescales of variation all mashed together. It is part of who I am to visualize reality in this way, thinking in the graphs I love.

I have been teaching for a sufficient time to recognize that these visualizations—graphs of changing variables stretching out in every direction—aren't everybody's thing, nor is the concept of Poisson counting statistics. If you prefer to collapse all this data rambling into "there will be ups and downs for nearly everything and that variation occurs on all sorts of timescales and is subject to the vagaries of randomness," nobody would blame you, but it could be worth remembering that some things that look like important spikes or dips might be merely random fluctuations resulting from counting statistics or "noise," and it is unhelpful, maybe occasionally dangerous, to read nonexistent patterns in that noise, extrapolating those nonexistent patterns into broad, sweeping models of reality. Humans, however, are built for recognizing patterns and making meaning, leading to reading nonexistent patterns in noise being one of the things at which we are particularly adept. We do it so well that it has been given a name—apophenia.

If a few recent years could be characterized by the blessing of plenty, then this year and the one coming two years later are surely years of paucity. In a typical year among the twenty-two we are tracking, I bagged as many or more birds than I did in these two leaner years combined. It was a second consecutive pheasantless year. The grouse population was continuing to evaporate, without my even getting a shot at one. Perhaps the most startling marker of the decline was that I managed to bag (although I shot two, as we see in a moment) a single wood duck, the only duck of any kind I got. Over the years, as grouse became less central to my hunting and woodcock were too rare and precious to take more than one or two, there was a sizable stretch of time between an opening flurry of rail and snipe (and later dove) hunting and the pheasant season getting underway at the end of October. Ducks did such a good job filling that void that I started building much of the hunting year around them, always managing to get a few, usually several.

My outdoor journal from the current year offers little help in deciphering what was going on; the hunting appears to be about the normal amount in the normal places. It may be best not to work too hard at trying to understand one or two down years, the equivalent of finding patterns in noise or fretting over what you have done wrong to get only a single orange M&M in a sample of twenty-four. I likely was barely in the wrong place at the wrong time and didn't quite connect. On a couple of days, if I had decided to go to place A instead of place

B, or if I had turned left into the cover instead of right, the whole year might have taken on a different character.

All was not tumult and disaster. I shot well at snipe, flushing them regularly, and while chasing snipe I shot my first ever sora rail. I felt a bit conflicted about taking the life of something that provided so little sustenance and to a degree I still do, but rails have become a fixture of my hunting year, providing a usually reliable way to get back into the hunting game. Rail hunting affords me the opportunity to see plenty of birds and soak everything in while roaming the marsh just as the calendar turns to September. Finally, I got my woodcock for the year, but that proved a challenge.

I was attempting to jump ducks along a remote trout stream at a property that had, in recent years, taken over from Old Homestead Place as my most reliable spot for both ducks and grouse. This mid-October day was slow, and I was far along the stream before woodies appeared, five of them bursting off the water as I knifed in toward the stream from the cover of the adjacent woods. Jump hunting ducks is built on knowing your properties. Aware of all the places ducks were most likely to be, I cut through the woods to the stream strategically, alert for an explosion like the one I just encountered, hoping for one or two birds. When five come up, instead of achieving the necessary hard focus on a single bird, I tend to flock shoot, as I suspect I did here. Still, a bird dropped into the stream with a heavy splash.

A year earlier, I had shot a duck at nearly this exact spot. That bird had been very close, too close, with the shot likely to be ineffective or too effective, since there was no space for shot to spread sufficiently to afford a decent chance of covering the bird without many pellets hitting simultaneously and destroying the meat. Somehow, I defied the odds of those two extremes and knocked the bird down wounded. Despite it being no more than ten yards away when it went down, I lost sight of the wood duck the instant it hit the water, as if the bird had slipped through some crack into a different dimension. This stretch of stream is rife with undercut banks shielded by long grass. After twenty minutes of searching around where the bird went in, lifting a clump of overhanging grass revealed the duck far back in a cavelike undercut.

This year's bird was also wounded and much more trouble, as it landed twenty-five yards out, where the stream was about to make a hard left turn, causing the water to disappear from view. Still, I was confident, believing that I had deduced the secret of successful retrieves the year before. I worked the grassy edges from ten yards downstream of where the duck went in to twenty yards upstream before I meticulously worked the stretch again and again, making my way farther upstream with each pass. My last-ditch effort was to slowly walk upstream in case the bird had managed to work against the current to hide an unexpectedly long way away.

Exasperated, I was nearing the end of the line, where the stream would meander onto private land. When I stopped to weigh the merits of crossing the stream to push the final fifty yards of public land so far upstream from where the duck fell, a woodcock twittered off the stream bank eight yards to my left and angled across the water, slicing back my direction toward a lovely plateau there. As usual, I threw the gun to my shoulder and fired too quickly, but there was time to breathe and make a good second shot that dropped the bird in the beauty that lay beyond the creek. There is no way that having that woodcock in the game bag could erase the sting of a wounded duck out there somewhere, a sting I know all too well. Still, it was a woodcock in the game bag.

No matter how well one understands the vagaries of Poisson counting statistics and the folly of overinterpreting noise in data, it's natural, even if not exactly reasonable, to ask what one might do differently in the year ahead to precipitate a more favorable outcome. In my case there was only one logical answer to that question: buy a new gun. My new gun, a 16-gauge over/under, from the "fine gun room" of a large outdoor retailer, felt light and responsive but not insubstantial. In terms of cost and quality, it might be best thought of as a midrange gun, and low midrange at that, instead of a genuinely fine gun, but having shot mass-produced pump guns my entire life, it felt like a functional work of art in my hands. My only concern with the gun was whether I could get accustomed to the double triggers, one trigger for the top barrel and one for the bottom barrel. It turns out that I maybe should have been more focused on what the dealer said to me (only after I had made the purchase of course): "If it doesn't fire when you pull the trigger, no need to bring it back. Just spray a little dry lube in the trigger mechanism and shake it out."

Humans can be remarkably adaptable, and I adapted to the double triggers quickly. In fact, now that my primary gun has a selective single trigger, I miss the double triggers. I grew proficient at sliding my finger to the back trigger when the tighter choke was called for but have never gotten the hang of moving the selector on the safety of my newest gun, although I do occasionally inadvertently change barrels while disengaging the safety. For sure the new gun didn't fix any of the bad shooting habits I had acquired over a lifetime, but I shot pretty well with it. As always, there were days of not-so-good shooting and days of better shooting, but the better days were reasonably plentiful, the gun helping me most later in the day during long outings. I was in my forties now, having more or less failed to notice that occurrence, but subtle signs of aging had crept into my life, and this new, lighter gun meant less fatigue at the end of a long day afield, with better shooting the result.

It was a few years before trouble appeared on a cold steel-gray day, the Wednesday before Thanksgiving, with a bite that brought to mind the Eagles' "Desperado" because there was no sunshine, but for most of the day the sky stubbornly refused to snow. The students were gone for the holiday, and I took the afternoon off to look for pheasants. Walking the brush rows bordering leased cornfields on our public land, I had the kind of luck that swings way out past good on the statistical tail, reaching almost unbelievable when a rooster got up fifteen yards in front of me on my side of the brush row. This is a sort of miracle when it occurs because wild birds always know to get up on the far side, screening themselves from danger. When I drew on the bird, my trigger pull was greeted with a not-so-satisfying "click" from the gun. Things had been so perfect with this flush that I was able to bag the bird with the second barrel. Inspection revealed that the first trigger pull had dented the cap of the shotgun shell but not sufficiently to make it go boom. Since the shell was from what was for me a new manufacturer (16-gauge ammunition can be "take what you find") and so much time had passed since the gun dealer's warning, I figured it was merely a defective shell. As I walked down the hill, the weather defied Don Henley and the sky did snow.

After that first time, failure-to-fire incidents started occurring, but sufficiently infrequently that I more or less forgot about them between trips to the field. One of the more interesting failures occurred when I was crawling up a very steep bluff, headed for a clear-cut on top, hoping to scare up a woodcock or maybe a grouse, despite grouse being essentially gone by that point. The rustling above me was a familiar one, arising from a flock of foraging turkeys. They were located where the bluff was transitioning from nearly vertical into nearly flat, a turn of topographic good fortune that meant I could sneak in very close before they saw me. When they did see me, the flock had the sort of chaotic scatter that is the dream of the fall turkey hunter who wants to grab a seat and call them back in, except I wasn't turkey hunting and didn't have my calls. One bird flew twenty yards up into a tree to my left and perched, craning its neck, attempting a glimpse at what had caused all the commotion. I was choked as wide open as it gets, cylinder and improved cylinder, but this bird was close enough that I thought the improved cylinder and my lightweight 7 ½ lead shot might do the trick, despite the spread of the shot being too much and the weight of the pellets being not enough for ideal. I eased the gun up, settled on the bird's head, and pulled the back trigger, resulting in a disappointing click. Nearly vertical shots were more likely than others to result in failure. Somehow the turkey was still sitting there looking at me. Was cylinder choke OK? I guess. So I pulled the front trigger and prepared to reload in a hurry if I needed to follow up. The bird displayed no initial reaction to the shot before rolling off its perch stone dead, landing with a thud below. The next week, I was talking to a bow hunter in the lot as we were getting ready to head into the forest and developing a strategy that would keep us from wandering into one another, less of a problem for me but not great for someone hoping to keep their presence concealed from wary deer. I knew his truck had been in the lot the week before. I described my turkey hunt, and he said, "Yeah, I was up on top of that hill when the turkeys scattered. It was something to see one fall from a tree."

This intermittent gun failure lasted two or three years before the problem worsened to the point of vexation. The gun needed work. I didn't know a gunsmith, which was as good an excuse as any to acquire another gun, one that has served me well since I retired that 16-gauge.

When I see it, I feel a bit of shame and know I must find somebody to work on it. I'd love to use it again.

This attention to guns, maybe like attention to dogs, certainly akin to attention paid to shooting performance, runs the risk of turning one's focus from the birds to the hunter, but nothing is ever quite as simple as it seems when we first look at it. When I was in graduate school, people were fond of calling the fact that most of the matter in the universe is dark matter and that the dark matter had to be nonbaryonic the "ultimate Copernican revolution." We recognize the need for dark matter to exist because of its gravitational pull on visible objects like individual stars in galaxies and individual galaxies in clusters of galaxies. Adding up all the inferred mass from the observed gravitational pulling leads us to deduce that maybe 80 percent or more of the mass in the universe is dark matter, stuff we don't see directly but the existence of which we infer because *something* is pulling on the stuff we see. We call the matter we do see baryonic because almost all of its mass comes from protons and neutrons, each of which belong to a class of particles called baryons. One reason we think the dark matter is not made of baryons is that it would simply be hard to hide that much normal matter as dust or gas or brown dwarf stars. We've gotten pretty good at rooting those things out and seeing them one way or another. More important, the total amount of baryonic stuff we see is consistent with what our models suggest was made in the Big Bang. The density of baryons a few minutes after the Big Bang is just right to produce what we see in the universe now, and our model of the Big Bang is in solid agreement with other observations. So it's not a locked down 100 percent deal that the dark matter can't be baryonic and hiding someplace, but it's pretty unlikely and, recalling our discussion of noise and Poisson statistics and such, that's the best we can do. These slivers of uncertainty in science bother people sometimes, but I like to think of it like playing poker. If you have a hand that wins 90 percent of the time, you are always better off betting it. Sure, you will lose one out of ten times, and it will sting when you do, but in the long run, you will be far better off playing the 90 percent winners than just randomly betting every hand that comes along, guessing and hoping. For the scientist it is important to remember that the sliver of doubt remains and to be always true to it, even if the chance we are wrong in some instance is only, say, 0.1 percent , because every now and then, one time in a thousand on average to be precise, that unexpected thing will turn out to be correct. You gotta keep walking around that track.

The Copernican revolution moved Earth from the center of the universe, and the dark matter revolution suggests we aren't even made of the same stuff as most of the universe, hence the "ultimate Copernican revolution" moniker. Sometimes I worry when I teach a general astronomy course that it might feel all a bit demoralizing to students, the universe getting bigger and less anthropocentric with each new class day, humans feeling more and more diminished until we aren't even made of the primary stuff of the universe. So I remind the students that what has developed is an interesting tension, the human's place in the universe shrinking away, while the complexity and beauty of our understanding of the universe on such a grand scale could be nothing but a testament to the glory of humanity, evidence of human ingenuity, perseverance, and both need and ability to connect with something larger. It's possible there's something similar with hunting that I would be good not to forget in my push to ensure that the bird remains primary, a recognition that the hunter and the land bring their own beauty and are still key to the story of our coexistence on this planet.

Despite my "functional work of art" view of the new gun, I didn't pamper it, taking it out everywhere I went, even on rainy snipe hunts in the marsh muck. I grew proficient with the gun because I stumbled onto plenty of ducks. As usual in those days, I started the early duck season along the creek at Old Homestead Place on what was a pleasant enough morning that yielded a delightful hike along the creek, punctuated by short bits of leaning against trees near likely holes, but no birds. It wasn't far to a property that borders the river into which the Old Homestead Place creek flows, worth the short detour for a stop on the way home. I had visited this property, River Wetland Place, off and on for the past few years. Small puddles dimpled low areas of grass and sandbar willow thickets. By all appearances, rails and snipe should love it here, although I had never encountered one loving it. I was about to discover that in wet years, really very wet years, the place transformed into a watery paradise.

Walking along a dike that separated low land from the river, cotton-woods towering over the land between the dike and river on my right, spindly willows scattered about the lowlands on my left, I encountered a pool of water with a surface area about the size of and footprint of one or two modest houses. Blue-winged teal exploded from nearly every square inch of the surface, and I shot one on the rise, downing another from a small group that circled back by as they departed. Unfortunately, I was wearing rubber boots for hiking along creek bottoms, not waders for hunting pools. With two ducks to retrieve, there was no choice but to plunge into the scummy pool up over my belly button. This one tiny pond led to plenty of action for me and my new gun as fall unfolded. At one point, I had half a dozen decoys out on the little pool while calling to a wary mallard drake that looked as if he were about to leak away at the outer edge of visual range. I hit the call, and he circled back to look things over before widening the circle back out. This fun had lasted several minutes, when I had my back to the pool trying to turn the mallard one more time. The whoosh of a flock of teal landing in the decoys behind my back was unmistakable. Late summer had been wet. I'd read a DNR news story claiming things were likely to be tougher on duck hunters because with so much water, ducks could be wherever they wanted to be instead of where hunters wanted them to be. It was my good fortune that where I was and where the ducks wanted to be intersected neatly. But the line between good fortune and bad can be thin. The water that had held those ducks in place was still there the next summer, and to paraphrase Louis XV or Madame de Pompadour, "After this, the flood."

My first woodcock encounter with the new gun didn't go particularly well. It was a stunningly beautiful mid-October Thursday morning, a Thursday when I wasn't going to the office at all. Often in academic departments we have weekly colloquia, research presentations that allow us to interact with others in our field and get an update on work going on out there. This particular afternoon, I was delivering the colloquium presentation at a physics department a few hours to the northwest, explaining to the students and faculty there what I thought we had learned from all the graphs of LPV brightness we had studied. What better way to prepare for an academic presentation on long-term stellar variability than a morning looking for grouse and woodcock? I was hunting a property that holds what is almost certainly the most popular trout fishing stream in Iowa. Even then there were times one had to stay far away from the throngs, but now it is almost overrun, although I can still manage a hunt or two each fall. Let's call it Troutpalooza Place. We've already looked into the future to meet Troutpalooza Place because it is where my gun is going to first fail on the "Desperado" pheasant.

There is a utopian flat expanse that borders the creek. This expanse, holding scattered dense pockets of shrubs and short trees, rolls into a relatively gentle hill that sported a good clear-cut at that time. On my way to the clear-cut, I worked from cover pocket to cover pocket across the flat until I reached the point of intersection with hill, where three woodcock came out from under a single bush. They flew in well-timed succession. I didn't react quickly enough for the first. I missed the second and then missed the third. Managing to get one of the three back into the air, I missed again. We'll say it was the new gun, dismissing the data that we don't like—all those ducks already eaten or in the freezer from a dozen good shots.

The woodcock I bagged came from a clear-cut at Old Homestead Place, the clear-cut that lay across the farmer's road from the field entrance where I got my bird the day the conservation officer checked my license six years earlier. It was thick going, but the bird got up when I was where I could swing the gun.

The reader might have noticed my dad's presence less and less in these accounts. I hadn't noticed at the time. Of course, it's as I tell my students when we are discussing measuring our own Milky Way Galaxy, it's hard to measure the soup when you're in it. Likewise, it's challenging to see the story as it's unfolding. Each of the individual stars you see in the night sky is part of the Milky Way, also what we call the hazy band that runs from Cassiopeia in the north down through Sagittarius in the south (for us Northern Hemisphere folk). That hazy band is the flattened disk of our Galaxy. It's a little like standing in a woodcock woods, where you see individual trees relatively nearby but at some point, they merge into unresolved forest. You know, a "can't see the forest for the trees" kind of thing or maybe a "can't see the Galaxy for the stars" kind of thing. It took decades, many decades, of struggle and human inventiveness to determine that we live about twenty-six thousand light-years from the center of a galaxy that is about a hundred thousand light-years across.

Looking back, I can see this story better, I believe, but don't be fooled into thinking I put too much stock in the "hindsight is 20/20" myth. However challenging it is to discern the nature of the soup while backstroking through the broth, making meaning of the past is no sure thing either. The I Fight Dragons song "Rewind" serves as the theme for the popular television show *The Goldbergs*. In that song we are led to believe that, while the future remains a mystery, our understanding of the past gains clarity as we age. Surely, we are better at discerning the story when we are not in the midst of it, but we don't perceive it perfectly looking back either, being particularly susceptible to projecting what we want the story to be onto it. A real danger lies in our overconfidence in the belief that the past is clear and getting clearer every year, but that goes without saying because the real danger lies in overconfidence wherever it might lie.

My dad was slowing down. We couldn't hunt as frequently, as long, or in terrain as tough as we had in the past. When my parents visited, I started seeking relatively flat ground with cover that could be accessed without an enormous walk, all this happening while I was busy not noticing, such is the nature of the slow evolution of life. The result was less success finding and bagging birds. In fact, we started doing more trout fishing with each successive trip. The trips were even harder on my mom. In addition to her ever-developing Parkinson's disease, she'd had a stroke years earlier and the long car ride made her sick. With each year growing noticeably tougher on her, there was no way we could keep doing what we always had much longer.

My very first Iowa bird was a pheasant I shot during my second autumn in state, having been far too busy getting my feet under me in my new job to get out during the first fall. I joined two colleagues to hunt a few farms they knew in the area. One of these colleagues was from my academic department. The cycles of life were made clear when he noted that I arrived in the department at the same age he was when he became a member of the department. Further, a more senior member of the department had welcomed my colleague who was now welcoming me. My colleague's senior colleague was then the same age my colleague was now. To top it all off, my colleague's senior colleague is known for being the one who built our department. If we pay attention to these sorts of details, it is possible to see that history is not always as long as we imagine it. A final connection is that my colleague is the same age as my father. I am now four years shy of the age my colleague was when we first met.

The first rooster of my life was the only one we bagged that day, likely a young-of-the-year bird, on the smallish side and sporting a short tail. Adding to that likelihood is that it is the least aggressively flying wild pheasant I have ever come across. My first pheasant encounter left the impression, long since corrected, that pheasants were gaudy floating balloons.

My second Iowa bird was a beautiful drake wood duck taken from the creek that runs through Old Homestead Place. Given my history of only upland bird hunting, it's not a shock that my first duck hunting experience mimicked the upland experience, flushing ducks while getting shots as best I could at woodies weaving through the timber like grouse, as other ducks would be unable to do. In *With Wings Extended*, Hoch states, "Bellrose and Holm (1994) cite their unpublished data showing that wood ducks have the broadest wing relative to length of any duck. Long, narrow, pointed wings are ideal for straight, fast flight. Shorter, stubbier more rounded wings, like those of quail and grouse, are good for zigging and zagging, but not for long, sustained flight." Even though I've shot more than a hundred ducks since then, that first wood duck remains the only banded duck—the only banded bird—I have bagged.

North American ducks have been banded regularly for more than a hundred years. Other birds are banded as well, some in programs formally overseen by government agencies, some not. In his 1949 *A Sand County Almanac*, Aldo Leopold writes of banding chickadees, more or less for fun I think, learning, among other things, that those chickadees only very rarely reach seven years of age. According to the Ducks Unlimited website, tens of thousands of waterfowl are banded each year. Archived USFWS data from the year of my band suggests that 28,657 wood ducks were banded in the United States and 5,780 bands were recovered, 349 of them from Iowa. In addition to lifespan information, as with Leopold's chickadees, hunter-recovered bands help us learn when birds are where, our first, best understanding of migration routes coming from the timing and distribution of band recoveries. Woodcock are banded as well, with many of the same science goals as for ducks.

Nowadays, it is common for birds to be fitted with satellite transmitters so that migrations can be followed in live time. Picture a scientific model of woodcock migration making a specific prediction regarding when birds of what age will be where. Satellite data provides an empirical test of the model so that a refined model might emerge and make new testable predictions. Many of these live migration maps, including for both North American and European woodcock, are available, at least intermittently, online.

Wing collections are also done for many species. The USFWS website suggests that tens of thousands of duck wings, goose tails, and dove wings are received annually. The number of woodcock wings arriving each year is just under ten thousand. No mention of the number of rail wings. I have been submitting wings from each rail and woodcock I bag for many years. In the most recent year for which data is available, I submitted to the USFWS one of only two woodcock wings from the state of Iowa. In addition to the information that one gets from bands, wings provide sex and age data for each bird harvested, banded or not. It is good news, for example, when the ratio of young-of-the-year bird wings to mature bird wings is higher, implying a high rate of reproductive success that year. In his 2019 *Sky Dance of the Woodcock: The Habits and Habitats of a Strange Little Bird*, Hoch describes scientists gathering at a wingbee each year to extract data from all the woodcock wings submitted: "More than forty boxes packed with envelopes greet them. Before beginning, everyone takes a short quiz to refresh themselves on how to determine the age and sex of a woodcock from its wing. First-timers get a crash course before taking the test." Results from studies of woodcock can be found each year in the *American Woodcock Population Status*, ####, where #### is the year of report publication. In addition to the wing survey data, these reports contain information on singing-ground surveys, where trained observers drive specified routes and listen for male woodcock performing their mating calls (peents), and the Harvest Information Program, which surveys hunters regarding activity and success each year. The data suggest that the population in the central region of the United States is about 80 percent of what it was when I began hunting woodcock, not the catastrophic decline I have witnessed with Iowa ruffed grouse, but not a loss rate that can be sustained indefinitely. Graphs constructed from wing survey data covering the past six decades make it look as if nesting success has been lower during the time I have been hunting woodcock than it was in previous years. If nesting success drops, bird population totals must follow—the reason wet springs can be devastating for quail and pheasants. As a lover of numbers who hears music and narrative associated with data, being a tiny part of these results has added immense depth to my outdoor experience.

Each year, the Iowa DNR conducts an August Roadside Survey and publishes a report of the results, not entirely unlike the USFWS Woodcock Population Status reports. A graph of pheasant counts and pheasant harvest since 1962 shows pheasant numbers plummeting at one point. The report author has circled this drop while adding the note that it coincided with five consecutive very snowy years, a span we are in the midst of at this point in our story. My dad and I hunted together just two days this year, both short outings for pheasants while the pheasant population was crashing. The statewide pheasant population would eventually bottom out at about one-seventh of what it was when I shot that first rooster with my new colleagues, having since rebounded, but only to about half of what it was when Iowa pheasants and I were first introduced to one another. Still, what my dad remembers are these last few years of hunting together. In his mind the Iowa pheasant population will be forever at rock bottom. When I share with him that I flushed a rooster pheasant, he always responds that it must be some sort of miracle. I remind him that populations are back to levels that make it reasonable to encounter a bird here or there, even on the public land we hunt, but by the next time we talk it will once again be a miracle if I have seen a rooster. I suppose it is.

All the snow, added to the water that had given me special duck hunting the fall before, kept us balanced on a knife edge, with the ground saturated much of the spring of this year. We managed to ride things out until one big rain event in early June pushed us past the limit, and we experienced what people would at the time call a 500-year flood event, the probability of a flood that large being about 0.2 percent in any year. We would have another such flood eight years later, one that would hit the residents of the small town between my house and Arroyo Place particularly hard.

I am aware that where I live isn't ideal for everyone, but it has treated me well by providing an almost unimaginable variety of outdoor experiences within an easy drive as well as dark skies, fertile soil, little traffic, and lots of space. The best part may be my walk to work, two miles mostly through woods along the river that passes a few hundred yards from our house, providing some glimmer of solace to even the dreariest day. Summer evenings, we walk over to the river, aiming to catch a couple of fish as the last light fades, returning home through a rising wall of fireflies.

A dike separates our neighborhood from flood waters, and it did its job this year, keeping the river out, but the push of water overwhelmed the sewer system, and several inches of tainted water came up in the basement, ruining all the appliances there. File cabinets, shelves, and storage cabinets floated up, tipped, and dumped contents into the mess. Some of this I could have prevented had I not been out of town.

While a brief weekend in central Wisconsin was the only hunting road trip I ever completed with my father, fishing is a different matter. My family had gone to The Lake to fish and fish hard every year in June since the year before I was born, the week becoming the most important holiday of the year, surpassing those more widely known and celebrated. The annual June trip served as vacation year after year. Once, we took a July trip west to see Mount Rushmore, Yellowstone, and the Badlands. Another time, we spent two days exploring the museums of Washington, DC, and there were two very brief two-day trips to Gatlinburg, Tennessee, while I was growing up. Otherwise, vacation meant The Lake, and The Lake meant fishing. It is a lesson that I learned well, as to this day it is difficult for me to imagine a vacation that doesn't have at least a little fishing in it. Whenever I am traveling in the absence of fishing, I can't help but look at any body of water I pass and wonder what fish it holds and the best way to fish it.

When the flood arrived, I was with my parents at The Lake. With no wireless service at the resort, one must drive several miles toward town to get connected. When a call came in to the resort owners that my parents' neighborhood had been hit by a flood, I hurried to town to see what I could learn. Passing one magic curve on the road out to the highway, my phone started chiming as if it were on fire, reporting message after message. My parents' neighborhood had been hit but not their house. It was a surprise to learn it was my house, hundreds of miles from theirs, that had seen the flood.

I returned a call to the friend with whom I was hunting when we saw the eagle hawk a goose. His house had been hit much harder than mine, but he was trying to get into my house to assess the damage there. I gave him guidance to a key, and he and others had the water pumped out by the time I was back, but a lot of clean up remained. Among the more significant losses was a pair of ducks that had still been in the freezer. The new gun had been standing low enough that the water made it a couple of inches up the stock, leaving it largely undamaged, but to this day it bears the mark of that flood. Most of my shotgun shells were stored on the lowest shelf and lost. Still, so many people lost so much more, and we were one of the first communities hit as the floodwater worked south through the state, meaning that we started repairs earlier. It wasn't long before it was nearly impossible to get things like water heater control boards, so many had been destroyed so quickly. It was now that the first refrigerator was deposited at Refrigerator Bend Place.

The massive flood surely did nothing to help the pheasant population that was already struggling. The insult on top of the earlier injury was that the flood happened so early in the year that by the time hunting season rolled around, my duck hotspot at River Wetland Place was too dry to hold birds. Maybe I was fatigued from the year that had unfolded, or maybe it was just another random fluctuation, but this ended up being a year of things other than hunting success. Still, I managed to bag a woodcock on October 20, when I made a clean kill of the only one I saw that year, shooting it within yards of where I got my bird the year before, in the same clear-cut at Old Homestead Place. The USFWS wing survey report identified it as an adult male.

YEAR 10

Delighted by the Unexpected

Sometimes reflection allows one to recognize opportunities missed. Two years earlier, I had used a down year of hunting as an excuse to purchase a new shotgun. It's really hard to know why it didn't occur to me to repeat that again this year, following another down hunting year.

This was a year of first and, so far anyway, only experiences in the field. All in all, it was a quality rebound year, with the season's novelty largely centered on the marsh and ducks. Every few years in the process of shooting blue-winged teal, wood ducks, and mallards, I bag a green-winged teal. This happens often enough that the event is pleasingly familiar. Yet it's just enough out of the normal cadence of autumn for me to reflect a bit more appreciatively than usual when I have a green-winged teal in hand, especially when it's a brightly colored drake. This is the only year so far that I have bagged two, the pair arriving in my game pouch three weeks apart. There is a little corner of the marsh where I like to sit when I decoy ducks, a section that is away from most people, shallow enough to wade reliably, and possessing a natural tangle of brush for hiding, without my having to worry about building a blind. One morning, I got to the marsh late to get my dekes deployed just as legal shooting time arrived. When I turned around after returning to my brush tangle, there was a duck dropping into my spread, apparently oblivious to the fact I was standing there. This was so unorthodox that I actually wondered for a moment if I should pass on the shot, but I took it and was delighted with the green-wing. Three weeks later in the same spot, I got another in a more traditional way. What makes this all the odder is that I could have had a third in between those two. I had him on a string, calling quietly while he spiraled down toward the decoys. Without any advance notice that things were about to go sideways, the duck flared and disappeared. I looked down for the first time since beginning to work that bird and saw two hunters who were hunched over, slinking along the dike, stalking my decoys. I stood and said hello. The young, probably high school–age hunters said, "Heh, heh. Your decoys sure looked and sounded like real ducks over here," before trudging away.

Those three green-winged teal experiences would have been enough to make it a standout duck year, but what happened in the midst of those events pushed it to the edge of believability, something akin to pulling an orange M&M from a bag of Reese's Pieces. I love this marsh because it's relatively small and isolated, fifty miles from the big river and a long way from where the potholes start in earnest. Interesting ducks show up, particularly during the spring migration, but it is largely a blue-winged teal, mallard, and green-winged teal place, with the occasional wigeon, pintail, and such thrown in as an interesting surprise. Built into our academic calendar, somewhere around October 20, a prime time for much of the hunting I do, is our three-day fall break. It used to be common for me to take one morning of the break to sit over my tiny decoy spread in my tiny corner of the marsh for an hour to an hour and a half before bagging up the decoys and stashing them in the brush while I walked all over the marsh, working grass edges, cattails, and rushes. You can see that in this activity I maintain the soul of an upland hunter, feeling better when the legs are moving. I haven't done this long morning of marsh mucking for a decade. Maybe the marsh is more crowded now or I'm busier and don't want to spend an entire morning or maybe I'm older, and walking miles and miles in waders has lost appeal, or I spend more time doing other kinds of hunting. Who knows?

On these marsh walks, ostensibly I am hunting snipe. Most rails are already enjoying a buffet of Cajun seeds in Louisiana, at least as

I picture it. Ducks do flush from the rushes, but infrequently. One year, I shot a coot while traipsing, wanting to see if it was as foul as everyone claims. We had it in the pan mere moments before throwing open the windows in brisk November, airing the house for hours. I considered burying the pan in the back yard to be rid of the stench but feared it might defoliate the entire neighborhood. The dog thought it was heaven. I read once that in some parts of their range, bald eagles rely on coots for 90 percent of their diet. I'd think more of the eagles if they'd improve their diet by replacing coot with weeks-old roadkill.

But having birds in the vest doesn't lie at the heart of these mornings. If I may be so bold as to riff on Shakespeare, the walk's the thing wherein we see our spirit soar and sing. A walk through a marsh, not near a marsh or through the periphery of a marsh, but deep in the core of the place is unlike a walk anywhere else. Only there do I have the (presumably erroneous) sense of an entire rich, nearly undisturbed, ecosystem all around me. I could spend a full morning surveying seeds of plants I know nothing about, followed by an afternoon of crawling around examining gastropods, wondering if they were snipe food. But that kind of close inspection would lead to missing the grandeur of the openness, swirling swarms of blackbirds over the grass far in the distance toward the giant cottonwoods that demarcate marsh and river.

This morning, I had been kicking around the place a long time, flushing three snipe. I got one, missed one, and failed to get a shot at one—pretty typical stuff. I rounded the corner of a grass line where a small bay opened up in front of me, with the mouth of the bay blocked by my presence. Against the far back edge of the little cove swam a stunning drake canvasback, the only one I have ever seen, except in large rafts out in the middle of the Mississippi River. Needing the take-off space of a big diving duck, he had to come my direction. Against the far bank of the bay, he was a mere fifteen yards out as he passed. This was the kind of a once-in-a-lifetime shot I would surely choke, yet I did not.

Canvasbacks hold a special place in the collective imagination of waterfowlers. In "Hail to the King," in *Ducks Unlimited* magazine, T. Edward Nickens wrote, "The canvasback has been known as the king of ducks for who knows how long, and those of us who have pursued this wild, singular creature understand why it is so special. Part of it, for me, is because seeing canvasbacks is a rarity where I live, although there is a long historic connection to canvasbacks along the coastal sounds of my native North Carolina. Part of it is because the bird itself has such a stately air, with that blocky head and sloping brow, so regal in profile that it doesn't even need a crown to suggest a certain sort of royalty. Part of it is the canvasback's history, deeply woven in the fabric of waterfowling lore, science and conservation. Part of it is the fact that the canvasback, pardon the unscientific verbiage, is simply such a cool duck."

Twelve years later, I can feel the heft of that big duck in my hands, see those bold feathers—the black so black and the white dizzyingly white—and taste the orange sauce pepper duck from that Thanksgiving. I doubt I'll ever have another in hand; but again, who knows? A speaker at one of our opening convocations warned the faculty and students gathered to start an academic year against reading a story only for the big idea it might or might not contain. One might miss the myriad, beautifully intertwined smaller ideas. A big idea (not *the* big idea) might be woven into the thread that connects smaller ideas interspersed in stories of, say, the woods, prairies, and marsh. One idea contained in my canvasback story might be that if one puts in the time and pays attention, life has a breathtaking capacity to surprise. So I'll not say "never" about encountering another stunning drake canvasback or something else just as remarkable, but it was special enough for us to start calling the place it came from Canvasback Marsh.

Interacting with the canvasback was resonant with my observing auroras, the northern lights. The first, not quite only time I saw them was on the return to California from a Santa Fe conference trip I took with two of my friends, squeezed into my little pickup. It was quiet at Canyonlands National Park in the off season, and the ranger had desperately wanted to help us find interesting things to see and to tell us about the natural history of the place, as we were the only visitors around. I still feel a little bad that we wanted none of her expertise and obvious love for the place; we sought silence and solitude instead. It wouldn't have ruined our trip to let her talk to us for half an hour or so. That night as we tried to sleep in the cold desert air, waves of light impinged from the north, the aurora dancing across the horizon. A rare treat that far south, it resulted from a massive solar eruption that had made the spectacle visible to a much larger fraction of the United States than is typical for these events. We just happened to be in the Utah desert for it, much as I just happened to be in the right marsh when a wayward canvasback appeared.

A stream of charged particles flows from the Sun in all directions. We refer to this stream as the solar wind, and it consists mostly of protons and electrons, with an admixture of about 8 percent helium nuclei and tiny, tiny amounts of the nuclei of heavier chemical elements, including carbon, nitrogen, and oxygen. This solar wind pushed the tails of Comet Hyakutake and Comet Hale-Bopp, the two bright comets of my life, away from the Sun, just as the solar wind pushed the tails of Tyco Brahe's comet and all other observed comets away from the Sun. The solar wind gives rise to aurorae when it interacts with Earth's magnetic field. Most of the matter we encounter on a regular basis—oh, let's say a woodcock wing—is electrically neutral, consisting of huge numbers of positively charged particles, like protons, and an equal number of negatively charged particles, like electrons. Add an electron to a neutral particle, and it becomes a negatively charged particle. Remove an electron from a neutral particle and it becomes positively charged, like some of the sodium and potassium ions in our bodies. The charged particles arriving from the Sun have a difficult time passing through a magnetic field. Instead, they are shunted along the magnetic field, leaving any motion parallel to the field unaffected, while motion perpendicular to the field gets converted into circulation. Picture electrons hitting Earth's magnetic field largely pointing north-south, and electrons traveling north or south along that field while circling around it. Most of the solar particles get deflected right past Earth like stones skipped across a magnetic sea, while some build up in the Van Allen belts. When a larger surge of energetic particles, a coronal mass ejection, arrives from the Sun, it disturbs Earth's magnetic field and forces trapped particles out of their trap, sending them on a helix toward one pole or the other. There, they hit the atmosphere and excite atoms and molecules, pushing electrons within the atoms and molecules into higher energy states. These so-called excited electrons, which can't stay long in higher energy states, emit light we see as aurorae when they return to lower energies. Sometimes that light can be seen all the way down in Utah or Iowa.

The very best aurora I ever saw was from the bridge spanning the river by my house one November when my parents were visiting, sheets of light undulating above the bluff to the north, building, shifting, and dissipating before rebuilding into a shimmering curtain of light. I tried to convince my parents to make the short walk up to the bridge to see this likely once-in-a-lifetime appearance of the northern lights. Alas, settled in for the night, they were having none of it. Twice more, I have seen aurorae from Iowa, but they were easily missed faint glows along the horizon. The two better ones I have witnessed were such moving and haunting visual events that I could imagine, despite my affinity for seeking beauty close to home, pushing far north for two weeks one winter to chase aurorae every night. These relatively rare events are all the more able to touch the soul when one reflects on the astronomical scale of the journey of the particles creating the show.

The green-winged teal trifecta and breathtaking canvasback drake should have been enough for one autumn, right? But there was one more first and only. Remember this is a slowly unfolding tale of a life spent

with woodcock, not ducks. Well, OK, also ducks—ducks and woodcock and stars. Before the day that shall henceforth be known as the Miracle of the Canvasback, spoken of only in hushed terms, and before the first green-winged teal day, I had already encountered a woodcock a couple of times at Arroyo Place. About halfway down the length of the dry run from where I typically enter off the road used by farmers and the DNR, there is a sizable growth of buckthorn. Whatever problems these plants cause, I have found that woodcock love to sit beneath them. I had always imagined woodcock enjoying sitting under these shrubs because they hold green leaves after most everything else is bare, but then I saw a presentation of results from a student research project that aimed to assess whether earthworm infestation was higher in the presence of buckthorn, the shrub and the worm each being invasive in northern forests. I began to wonder about that possible connection instead, despite the inconclusive nature of the results being reported. In the great scheme of the flow of time, it wasn't all that long ago that there were no earthworms up here where I hunt. Somehow, woodcock managed without this dietary staple. Maybe somebody has an idea, but I certainly don't know how woodcock populations hundreds or thousands of years ago compared to what we have now. Were there fewer when they had to rely on other protein sources in the north, or were there as many or more, earthworms having more or less become a food of convenience? It seems likely that woodcock habitat use would have been different. Where might I have hunted woodcock compared to where I find them today? Not too long ago, the northern US was covered in ice, and woodcock were always to the south. Of course, it turns out that woodcock just love particular spots, birds piling into specific cover, buckthorn or not, and I might be overinterpreting my personal experience with woodcock and buckthorn, reading a pattern in what is essentially noise. In *Sky Dance of the Woodcock*, Hoch writes: "Woodcock also key in on some really small features of the landscape during migration. There are numerous reports in the literature stating that hunters can expect to find them not only in a particular area, but they can often flush them from the exact same location where they had previously flushed them." He then goes on to share several such reports. It appears that, as usual, my experience, while uniquely my own, has much in common with humanity across space and time.

On my first encounter, the woodcock got up in this buckthorn thicket and escaped, fully screened by the leafy bushes. Knowing generally where the bird had gone, I managed a shot when it flushed again, but the bird came out like a rocket flying low and banking right, so I never caught up with it. A week later, a woodcock was so close to where the one had been previously that I am pretty certain it was the same bird under the exact same bush. Once again, I didn't get a shot on the initial rise, although this time I did get glimpses of the woodcock through the thick cover. The bird sat through my efforts to get it back into the air.

I had returned to the arroyo another week or so later, having bagged my first green-winged teal and the canvasback in the meantime. The arroyo cover is about thirty or forty yards across for most of its length, with the typically dry creek bed cut several feet below the wooded perimeter. On the road side of the cover lies an expanse of prairie grass that yields the occasional pheasant. Beyond the other side of the arroyo, some grass stretches to distant forest. The grass is interspersed with cornfields that get moved around from year to year, and now that doves are legal game in Iowa, sunflowers are also planted in varying spots. About three quarters of the way to the end of the arroyo, the corn and sunflower fields yield to a forested hill, and the woodcock cover spreads, doubling its width but thinning out. This third time into the cover for the year, my bird came up before I had reached the dense buckthorn stand, and I made a clean kill shot as it arced toward the open prairie on the road side of the arroyo. A few minutes of searching the tall prairie grass yielded the beautiful dead bird and a promise of rumaki or another Thanksgiving appetizer.

Having not let the bird get the best of me for a third time, I pondered turning back through the prairie and heading home. It was not yet pheasant season, but I thought I might cut through the arroyo cover and take a look at the interior corn, supposing it possible I might bump a turkey from the edges. Three steps back into the cover and another woodcock flushed. Five steps later, two got up together. With that apparent abundance, I decided maybe I could go ahead and take a second bird. Late making the decision, I missed. As I worked the cover, birds kept popping up at regular intervals, and I missed twice more before I connected on my second bird. With two birds certainly sufficient, I walked around flushing woodcock without raising the gun again. Every now and then, I wonder if maybe I should have gone ahead and filled my three-bird limit, given that it was likely the best chance I'll ever have to do so. Surely, a migration event had occurred between my trips, landing me in what is known as a fall of woodcock. It's the only time I have experienced one. Having failed to count, I estimate twenty-five to thirty flushes happened in less than an hour that day. It's impossible to be certain how many distinct birds were represented in those flushes, but it was no fewer than eight, given where the birds were and how many came up together. Probably it was more like fifteen or eighteen. In any event, I could have taken another bird without damaging the population much, but population damage wasn't a big idea in this story. Having the rare pleasure of wading through a sea of woodcock was a bigger idea. The USFWS reported that both birds I bagged were young-of-the-year females.

YEAR 11

Beginnings and Endings

A few memories from the parcel of land that contains Grandpa Place, where my mom grew up, persist from when my grandparents still lived there, including once catching a large frog that ate the worm I dangled by the weeds while fishing with my grandfather. One morning, my grandfather and I were bringing eggs back from the hen house as I tossed mine up in the air carelessly. He said more than once, "Be careful. You'll drop that egg." He knew I would drop the egg when he gave it to me. I made it almost all the way in before it hit with a splat. He laughed and laughed. Of course, he would be the one an egg short at breakfast. He was a jolly sort whose sunny disposition shone through any clouds, and my mom used to tell me that the only time she ever saw her parents argue, even a bit, was the sole time they tried to hang wallpaper together. That recollection was about as dire a warning as my mother ever offered me. My mom's father passed away when I was about six years old, and her mother followed five or six years later. After my grandfather died, my grandmother lived with us. With dementia settling in, she would chase imaginary pigs around the house and hold conversations with people who had been dead fifty years. Once she passed, the Grandpa Place land went to my parents and various aunts, uncles, and cousins.

We lived in town, some twenty-five miles from the properties "in the country" where my parents were raised. "In town" is relative, of course, given that it was a big deal when city water and sewer became available in our neighborhood. For the entire time I lived there, it was a ten-minute walk to working farm fields of corn and soybeans.

Still, there was more light in town than in the country, and when I was old enough, I escaped to the Grandpa Place property to observe the night sky, including one August, another five or six years after my grandmother was gone, when I drove out to watch the Perseid meteors, taking along my cheap telescope. Meteor showers occur the same time each year, the meteors all appearing to have originated from a single point when their trails are traced back across the sky. That point of origin for the Perseids lies in the constellation Perseus, hence the name. Any night you walk outside under a dark sky, you'll see the occasional meteor zip by, but their trails don't trace back to a single point on the sky. These random nightly meteors arise when Earth's orbit collides with debris knocked off rocky bodies in the solar system— asteroids, moons, planets, or simply material left floating around after the planets, major and minor, of the solar system were formed. When that material burns up as it passes through our atmosphere, we see a streak of light. The meteors in showers typically come from dust grains boiled off comets when the comets are heated as they near the Sun in their orbits, the dust grains falling into the same orbital pattern as the comet from which they were liberated. Each year we intersect that orbit at the same time and in the same location. Picture a tunnel of debris we plow through at the same point in each orbital circuit, that debris tunnel yielding the streaks of light we see in a meteor shower. The quality of the showers can vary depending on the density of debris and precisely how we intersect the tunnel in a given year, but the Perseids are consistently productive year after year.

The night I went "to the country" to observe the Perseids, the meteor shower did not disappoint, but it was the rest of the sky that particularly moved me, the stars sparkling against the inky backdrop, and the haze of the Milky Way spanning horizon to horizon. Not having probed the sky to any great extent previously, I was seeing objects for the first time, objects I located by simply looking up and letting them appear against the very dark sky or by scanning slowly with binoculars.

Open star clusters M6 and M7 in Scorpius were particularly pleasing
in my telescope that was more of a toy than anything else. Open star
clusters are groups of stars, most often consisting of a few dozen to a
few hundred stars, though they can have fewer or more. These clusters
exist in the flattened plane of our Galaxy, where each star in the group
was born at the same time from a single cloud of gas. Open star clusters
are important laboratories for studying how stars evolve because, given
their common origin, all the stars therein must have started out made
of similar stuff at the same time, meaning any differences in how they
evolve must come from something else, the mass of each individual
star being the most important driver. Clusters like M6 and M7 are close
and sparse enough that the individual stars appear distinctly, creating
an image of glittering jewels. Another open star cluster, M23, lies just a
short hop from the two I enjoyed observing that night. The tiny patch
of sky my students and I study by taking images night after night, year
after year, is centered on open star cluster M23.

The most breathtaking surprise of the night for me was the Andromeda Galaxy, appearing easily without optical aid, looking like an
elongated smudge of fluorescent paint, startlingly large and easy to see.
To this day, I am floored when I see it, impressed by how easy it is to
spot against any sky that hasn't been ruined by terrestrial light spilling
upward. I am humbled by the knowledge of what it is and reminded
of the night and place where I first set eyes on it. A hundred years ago,
debate raged over the nature of so-called spiral nebulae like Andromeda.
One idea was that these objects, looking smooth and starless, were
clouds of gas within our own Galaxy, the Milky Way, the entire universe being essentially indistinguishable from the Milky Way, a sort
of big galaxy–small universe theory. The other model held that these
were galaxies like the Milky Way but so distant that the integrated
light of tens or hundreds of billions of stars amounted to the faintest
smudges of light on the sky, no individual stars readily visible in any
of them, a sort of big universe–small galaxy theory.

Harlow Shapley became a leading proponent of the big universe–small galaxy model that was supported by many different pieces of evidence, including that these nebulae were found almost exclusively far away from the Milky Way's disk in the sky, as if our Galaxy had pushed them out there via some sort of galactic wind. This influence of the Milky Way is not conceivable if the nebulae were distant galaxies in their own right. A flare star, or nova, in Andromeda that appeared in 1885 also supported this model, since it would have had to be enormously luminous if Andromeda were so distant that hundreds of billions of stars melded into an unresolved glow. Some astronomers thought they saw the actual movement caused by the rotation of these objects, like garden pinwheels, something impossible if they were distant galaxies because they would be flung apart by rotational motion of a rate high enough to detect. These pieces of evidence in support of the model that held that the spiral nebulae were local clouds of gas instead of distant galaxies were so strong that most—likely nearly all—astronomers believed this to be the better model. This story then becomes a cautionary tale of how important it is to keep an open mind and to keep walking around that track of science even if the probability of a model being wrong seems minute.

Heber Curtis became a leading proponent of the big universe–small galaxy theory after the work of Vesto Slipher, a fellow native Hoosier I might note, showed that the distribution of the colors of light—the spectra—of spiral nebulae is the same as that of stars, as it would be if they were in fact made of stars instead of gas. Gas clouds would yield a very different distribution of light. Slipher's work also demonstrated that the nebulae were moving away from us at enormous speeds, so fast that we should also see them moving across the sky, if they are in the Milky Way. But they don't show any hint of motion across the sky. In some ways, I think of Slipher as the Brahe of this story, so impressed am I with the quality of these observations that stretched the available technology—cameras, photographic plates, telescope drive motors—to its groaning, straining limit.

Edwin Hubble settled the question by finding a variable star in Andromeda while searching for novae similar to the one observed in 1885. Years before Hubble's work, Henrietta Leavitt had found that certain types of pulsating stars get brighter and dimmer with a very regular period of oscillation and that the time between their brightest and dimmest point or two successive brightest points is related to how much light they are emitting. If you know how bright something actually is, like a 100-watt light bulb, and how bright it appears (the light bulb appears dimmer in a predictable fashion as you move away from it), you can tell how far away something is. Hubble was able to use Leavitt's work to show that Andromeda was so distant that it couldn't possibly be part of the Milky Way. And Andromeda is the nearest of the big spiral nebulae, most of them existing at nearly unfathomably larger distances. We didn't see them along the plane of the Milky Way because the material of our Galaxy blots them out. The flare star in 1885 had been a supernova, an object not well understood at the time and brighter than most had thought possible for a star. As for the apparent rotation, it wasn't real. Perhaps astronomers were projecting what they expected or hoped to see on these objects. In the end, it's possible that the biggest impediment to our recognizing that the spiral nebulae were distant galaxies was a failure of imagination, the universe being so much larger than we could conceive. Beyond its enormous scale, the universe, including our tiny slice of the world nearest us, has an almost infinite capacity to surprise and delight with beauty, complexity, simplicity, variety, and anything we aren't attuned to or looking for.

This year, a special weekend started at a place we will call New Grandpa Place. It had become my favorite duck and snipe property and would soon be one of my best woodcock properties, with other birds there as well. It was at New Grandpa Place that I would use the cylinder barrel of my failing gun to take a turkey from a tree. The property is another very large one for our area. Right next to the highway lie boggy lowlands that always hold water, even in the driest years. A trout stream runs east of there, and east of the stream, heavily wooded hills rise to flat expanses of corn and grass, a microcosm of northeast Iowa outdoors, not unlike Old Homestead Place. Hunting the marshy area rates high on my list, with nobody else ever around because of the challenge of getting into it. Often I start the day by pass shooting ducks as they come off the biggest pool. Then I might kick around for snipe or set up decoys to see what ducks come back in. One morning, I was back at the parking lot after a thoroughly unsuccessful duck hunt, heading for a different big hill by a different trout stream, where I would turn the day around when I shot a pheasant. The following day I would catch one of the largest rainbow trout I have ever landed, six to eight pounds. Each of these is an interloper, not native to Iowa, and the difference between them could not have been starker. The pheasant rocketed out of low grass with a companion, both hell-bent on making it to the wooded fence line and the chance to run unimpeded for a mile. Wildness oozed from this bird as I held it in my hand. The oversized trout, by comparison, was sluggish, overfed, and lethargic, nothing about it exclaiming wild and free. Still, getting that fish out of the water without a net, on four-pound test line was a challenge that had to be comical for Kristin to watch. All I could do was roll it onto the mud, "waller it," as I was taught to say, its flopping sending mud spraying all over me.

In the parking lot, after my unsuccessful New Grandpa Place duck hunt, I met a young man going trout fishing. He explained that this property had belonged to his grandfather before ownership transferred to the DNR. I attempted to convey how special this place was to me and how grateful I would always be for his family's willingness to share it with the rest of us. I don't know if he understood, it being one of those situations when words can't quite capture the depth of what you intend, especially words between two strangers bumping into one another in a parking lot.

Another great day began at New Grandpa Place. I fought my way to my post several tens of yards off the pool, listening to the dozens of wood ducks loudly starting the day. Just after legal shooting time, they began boiling off in waves. I missed the first couple of shots but then dropped a stunning drake woodie that I located without much trouble, not always the case in the very thick marsh grass. After all the birds were off the pool, I kicked around and flushed a couple of snipe, missing the first and downing the second. Sometimes, making a shot that isn't a clean kill can actually be helpful. Snipe are particularly challenging to find in the heaviest part of the marsh. This one had enough life left to try escaping when I approached but not enough life left to get the job done. Two is about as many birds as I shoot any day, but I was interested in seeing about keeping the woodcock streak alive, and since the drive home took me near Troutpalooza Place, I swung in for a quick look at the clear-cut there. After a birdless hike to the top of the hill, motion to my right caught my eye. Two turkeys were walking along the outside edge of the forest, apparently unconcerned with my orange-clad presence there. Once again, I faced questions about whether I had sufficient firepower for the job, but the birds were only twenty-five yards away. When I pulled the back trigger, the turkey I had selected disappeared from sight, folded next to a log. This was likely a young-of-the-year bird, as its size was somewhere between nominal pheasant and nominal turkey.

After my parents arrived a week later, my dad and I hunted pheasants on both days of opening weekend. I'd like to report that we managed to get my dad a bird because this was to be the last time we hunted together in Iowa. A rooster got up in front of him, but he was unable to determine hen or rooster and didn't fire. One evening, when my father was in the other room, my mother told me that he had fallen asleep twice while driving up, and she had to shout him awake. She also looked utterly bedraggled from the drive. The message was clear. This was the last of these visits. He was unlikely to listen to her, so I would need to make sure the end happened. We weren't inclined to tackle difficult subjects head on, and we didn't this time. The next year I was able to travel to Indiana in the fall, heading off their potential trip to Iowa. The following year, I had a new job as associate dean that limited my time in the field, which meant we could pretend that's what was preventing their heading north for a visit. By the next year, our annual Iowa hunts were enough a thing of the past that we could simply move on. This evolution was made easier because by that time it had become clear to my dad that my mom's health had deteriorated sufficiently to preclude the drive. We celebrate retirements and other changes in life, but the most important things often just fade away, as they must because we're rarely certain when the end is the end, and even when we are sure the end is the end, it's often too painful to admit it's the end.

I found myself on the last day of woodcock season without my bird. Now, this wasn't unique, but it was uncommon. Fate smiled benignly on me—I was able to take the morning off for a hunt that day. I tried to turn my back on fate. Unfathomably in retrospect, I chose to hunt Canvasback Marsh for ducks that morning instead of visiting a woodcock woods. Likely it was some practical streak that led me there. I had hunted the woodcock coverts hard in recent days without a flush or seeing any whitewash birds had excreted. It's also likely I had to teach at 11:00, and the best duck action happens in the half hour before woodcock hunting is even legal. Also, the marsh had provided very interesting hunting experiences in the weeks leading up to the close of woodcock season.

Whatever led me there, I found myself in my little corner, watching and hearing the marsh come to life. The unexpected sounds of wood ducks getting ready for the day originated diagonally across the pool. Most wood ducks were long gone, and this marsh was on the edge of the prairie. Large trees were confined to the banks of a river some ways off. I rarely see wood ducks out on this open expanse. I was suddenly excited by a novel opportunity; if I bagged a wood duck, it would be my first from this property and the latest in the year I had ever gotten one. As the ducks got up, I gave them one quick call. Woodies being woodies, I knew my calling and dekes held little appeal, but I hoped to arouse a bit of curiosity. Indeed, they came my way. True to form, they didn't slow as they buzzed the tiny spread, but they swung by close enough.

When I shoot a bird and it goes silent, the first thing I feel, always, is loss, it having become critical for me to feel that brief tinge, that sudden absence. When I wound a bird, the feeling is something entirely different, and my heart sank to the boots of my waders when after my shot, the small flock banked hard left while a lone bird, my bird, curled out right, wings set, gliding and gliding and gliding. The bird settled into the thickest part of the cattails 120 yards away, very much alive.

It was hopeless, dog or no dog, a situation made hopeless by my poor shooting. Had I picked up the decoys, walked to the truck and driven home, my chances of finding that bird would not have changed noticeably. Yet search we must. I circled those cattails and kicked for forty-five minutes until my burning legs could take no more and I headed for the easiest way out. The fastest exit from the cattail nightmare was through a small willow thicket that led to a dike. When at last I broke free into the edge of the thicket, I paused to catch my breath. What wonders that pause can bring. When the woodcock erupted at my feet, I didn't raise my gun. Perhaps it was surprise or fatigue; likely it was that one never raises a gun at the appearance of a mirage or ghost. I gathered my wits, slowed my breathing, and walked the fifteen yards to where the bird had landed. The thicket was so tiny that there was nowhere for that bird to go but out over the open marsh, making it one of the easiest woodcock shots I had ever made.

By now I have shot my share of woodcock from sandbar willow thickets along marshy edges, but never so far from bigger woods or in a thicket so sparse and small, in a place that is more cattail marsh and rolling prairie than anything else. All that suggests I should exclaim that this was the most special woodcock ever, but every woodcock is the most special ever. Maybe there was more magic in the land than usual that day. On the wind I could sense the universe talking to me, saying something like, "You have made an honest effort here today. You have been true to both the ducks and the woodcock. Remember to be more careful next time. Here is this year's woodcock for you. Appreciate all that it is." Was it a perfect day? Most would say no. What it was, was hunting, with all its highs and lows, gains and losses. Maybe that does make it perfect.

YEAR 12

Continuity and Discontinuity

One of the things that going afield regularly each fall to hunt or all year to fish does is reinforce the sense of continuity, the image of our wheel rolling forward reappears. Returning to the classroom each fall and taking images of our little patch of sky night after night and year after year only adds to this feeling. We have been careful to recognize that the universe is ever evolving so that we are not returning to the same reality each year, but there are sudden, typically small, changes that happen routinely as well. We can think of these as discontinuities or "steps," a point in time where what comes before doesn't translate smoothly into what comes after. This year, such a step appeared in my outdoors life when Iowa introduced its first dove season and the small gray birds were scattered everywhere. A quarter of my birds for the year were doves, and they have become a regular part of each autumn for me, adding another small bird to the mix of each evolving fall, with a burst of dove hunting right as the calendar turns to September, then often another burst as we work deep into November. Mostly, I hunt them the way I would anything else, by walking them up. Hunted that way, they offer quite the wing shooting challenge because they don't typically let one get close before flushing. Often, after the flush, birds will zip around here and there, and a slightly better shot presents itself. Following this chaos is when my dove hunting most resembles what people who know of such things are likely to picture for a dove hunt as I hunker into whatever cover I have and wait twenty or forty minutes for scattered birds to return. This first year, my best spot was the cornfield where I shot that goose years earlier. The corn had suffered terrible wind damage, with large sections knocked flat amid standing corn. It was these flattened sections the doves preferred. I also found them at Canvasback Marsh, Arroyo Place, and Troutpalooza Place.

Doves have always seemed like game to me, even before there was a season in Iowa, and there was never a season in Indiana when I was growing up. In those early days ruffed grouse were the only game birds I saw with regularity. On the odd occasions that my dad and I stumbled onto a covey of quail as we cut across Grandpa Place from one grouse cover to another, he never failed to remark, "Must be birds those guys from Indianapolis [my uncle's friends] had down here for training dogs," so sure was he that wild quail were extirpated from our area. I now know wild quail were struggling in that area, but they weren't gone, and those hard-flying coveys we launched were almost certainly wild. In any event, ruffed grouse and bobwhite quail were the only gamebirds I knew for the first thirty-three years of my life. Pheasants and ducks came naturally, rails not so much. Even after having hunted them for fifteen years, flushing a couple hundred maybe, my brain still tends to say "not game" when the first one or two fly each fall. That's never been the case with doves. Before we had a season, when I was out scouring the fields and woods, I wouldn't flinch when a crow or a blue jay or a hawk or a robin or whatever flushed near me. But if a dove came up at my feet, something about the sound and the flight made my brain scream "Game! Game! Game!" the gun rising halfway to my shoulder before I got it checked.

A discontinuity occurred in my data acquisition life this year as well. One reason we undertake the project of focusing on a single patch of sky, the same 1,650 stars, for decades is that by using the same equipment from the same site continuously, we are able to detect subtler evolution of stars than if we were attempting to stitch together data sets widely separated in space and time and acquired by an array of equipment that varied dramatically from instrument to instrument. We are, of course, fooling ourselves to an extent because the equipment

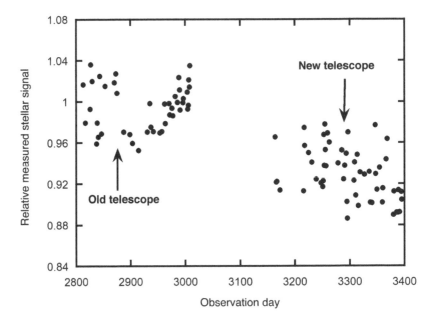

was always aging (telescope mirrors oxidizing, for example), and the atmosphere above us is never the same from one night to the next or one observing season to the next. Still, we expect to do a better job doing long-term monitoring this way. Alas, equipment breaks. We repair it as best we can, but eventually it must be replaced, and near the end of this year our telescope needed replacing. We began the following year with a new telescope, and the result was discontinuity, steps in measured star brightness as the accompanying graph shows so beautifully for a star chosen more or less at random from our population of stars.

Some stars, like the one in the graph, appeared to get a few percent fainter; some appeared to get a few percent brighter, and some stayed about the same. Our task was to figure out why and eliminate this artifact from our data because this kind of discontinuity throws quite a wrench into the works of looking for subtle changes in stars. We were guided in our effort by the realization that the new telescope had better imaging than the old. That is, the star images suddenly became smaller. Given that the new telescope did a much better job of transmitting blue light than the old telescope did, it was also possible that the equipment change caused bluer stars to suddenly appear brighter relative to redder stars.

We explored the ways our technique for measuring how bright a star is might be affected by star image size, either by some signal being excluded from the measurement as the star image gets larger, or by starlight bleeding in from neighbors because our field is very crowded with stars. Tighter star images might mean less bleed-in, resulting in steps. If our data calibration worked differently on bluer stars than it did on redder stars, the observed discontinuities could result when, suddenly, the bluer stars looked brighter than they had before because more blue light was getting through the system.

Generations of bright, hard-working students have struggled with this issue, without satisfactory resolution to the problem. An approach looks promising but then stalls, and we must back up and try a different route until the new path also chokes in around us; we back out of the thicket once more, and the process renews. I tell my students that doing science is much like writing poetry. Every minute detail matters, or as Depeche Mode once titled a song, "Everything Counts in Large Amounts." Whatever it is we're after won't reveal itself if we aren't persistent and attentive to every nuance. We are walking around that track of science, building a model of what might be causing our data discontinuity, predicting a better outcome with a new approach, and testing that new approach. In this process, when a predicted result isn't borne out one must ask, "Did the model fail or did we do an insufficient job of measuring so that it only looks as if the model failed?"

Recently, by scanning graphs of data, we recognized, to our great surprise, that the size of the step in our data was tightly correlated to x pixel position our camera, a realization that led us to the discovery that our previous telescope suffered significantly from an optical aberration known as coma, and that this coma got worse as one moved to the right across the field of view, accounting for the observed step size dependence on x. Now we are not yet celebrating because we have been here too many times before, seeing success just ahead of us before everything comes crashing down. I have noticed that sometimes people think that science works in a way that when an answer to a problem is found, the answer is obvious, like a light is illuminating it from above. Maybe it works that way for some people sometimes, but after so much struggle, a gnawing self-doubt persists. Have we fixed the calibration issue sufficiently so that if we want to make a claim that a certain class of stars gets brighter or dimmer by a percent or two over fifty years, we'll be confident to do so? There is no real rulebook; one must just decide when it is time to step into the abyss, and the history of physics is littered with both stories of those who lost Nobel prizes because they waited too long, unsure whether they had it right, and those who stepped too quickly, making an erroneous claim before they had all the bugs worked out.

If I have encountered those who have believed that solutions to scientific problems seem obvious at the time, then I have also talked with people who believe that hunting birds is easier than it actually is, and that it amounts to little more than the slaughter of animals that had no chance when confronted with the firepower a hunter brings to the field. Again, maybe it works that way for others, but I hope the stories I have related make it clear that this has not been my reality. Even without ever-present shooting struggles, I wouldn't be able to simply walk out and shoot some birds any more than, absent equipment trouble, I could shoot a few pictures of stars that would yield a thorough understanding stellar structure and evolution. I have worked to build models of where I think birds go and how they behave, testing those models with predictions of what will lead to a successful hunt, with the models failing that empirical test more often than not. Always, I must ask whether the model failed or whether I didn't give the model a sufficient opportunity to at least partially pass, becoming a qualified success. At least with our efforts to fix the steps in measured star brightness, the last of our old telescope data and the first of our new telescope data are unchanging, unlike the weather, the birds, and the world around.

In early October this year, I bagged a beautiful drake green-winged teal from New Grandpa Place at first light. A few minutes later, I shot a duck that I lost. It hit the ground with a heavy thump, but the poor light made it challenging to track the bird's descent into the marsh grass so that half an hour of scouring turned up nothing. The next week, after a quick visit to my parents in Indiana, I was kicking around the edge of the main pool at New Grandpa Place when a wounded mallard flapped out of the grass and skittered across the surface toward a willow thicket on the far side. I was able to stop its escape. Given that I've never seen another hunter at this nearly inaccessible place, I'm pretty sure that was my bird from the week before. I have only cleaned up my own mess later like that one other time, and it was within yards of where I fixed the mallard problem. I shot a rail by the pool, picked it up and admired it for a good while before dropping it in my game bag. Those big feet and green-yellow legs and beak are always striking in the hand. I skirted the pool until I reached a tiny hump of land where I sat in the cattails and waited an hour or two for ducks to fly in over my decoys. Back at the truck, the rail was missing from my game bag, just vanished. Poof! That was a Saturday. On Sunday, after pass shooting ducks as they came off in the morning, I returned to that hump of dirt, tossed out some decoys, and settled in. Only a few minutes into waiting, motion in the cattails caught my eye. It was a wounded rail attempting to sneak off. Again, I was pretty sure that was my bird. The whole time I was admiring it in the hand, it must have been knocked out or playing possum, if one can imagine a rail doing such a thing. Then it must have crawled out of my vest as I soaked up the sunshine, half-heartedly hunting ducks. That's the story I'm sticking to anyway.

By comparison, my woodcock this year was remarkably uneventful. I was in the clear-cut at Troutpalooza Place when the bird flushed about fifteen yards uphill. It towered sufficiently to give me a great look above the trees, and I folded it without incident, admiring it for a few minutes longer than I had the rail. This was also mid-October, and I flushed a grouse in that clear-cut on the same day. It was one of a few grouse I flushed that fall. Almost exactly a month later, I went back through the Troutpalooza cut and shot a grouse, likely the one I'd flushed with the woodcock. It was my last Iowa grouse. Almost exactly a month after that hunt, my dad, my childhood friend, and I were taking a slow stroll across Grandpa Place. We called it hunting because we carried guns, but we stuck to the easy terrain, covering minimal ground on mowed trails. It was the last time I was to hunt with my father.

YEAR 13
Wily Woodcock

It would be my hope that after our earlier Poisson counting statistics and graphing diversions you are well aware that measuring things is important to me, just as it is my hope that after a single scintillating classroom discussion, my students fully grasp the details of how electron degeneracy resulting from Fermi-Dirac quantum statistics leads to supernovae and thus the creation of all naturally occurring chemical elements found on the periodic table. But repetition and practice in different ways in different settings is an essential cornerstone of education. Not unlike going into the woods each fall, everything is the same but different, and we are different when we encounter something old anew. Even if some miracle of Poisson counting statistics allows the nearly impossible feat of two years being exactly the same, having the same encounter twice allows us to lock it in our brains while detecting subtle texture missed the first time around. So why not have another go at a dalliance with statistics, counting, and ranking here, right?

Let's begin with a digressional exploration of my use of the phrase "nearly impossible" when "impossible" would have been a better description as a result of the overwhelmingly large sample size of events in any year. At the heart of this matter lies the concept that there are two distinct kinds of impossible: strictly forbidden and statistically forbidden. Electric and magnetic phenomena are thoroughly explained by a set of rules known as Maxwell's equations. Some electromagnetic phenomena are strictly forbidden because they are not possible solutions to this set of differential equations. Given a particular electric current flowing in some region of space, for example, the strength and geometry of the magnetic field are defined by Maxwell's equations such that any other magnetic field cannot exist, so long as we have done a proper accounting of all electric currents and magnetic moments there.

The second law of thermodynamics, which tells us, among other things, that heat will only ever flow from hotter objects to colder objects and not colder objects to hotter objects, is an entirely different beast. The flowing of heat from cold to hot breaks no physical laws defined by differential equations like Maxwell's equations. Instead, this is related to the number of states or physical configurations that the system—say, the air in the room where you are now—can be in. As the number of particles involved goes up, the fraction of the total number of states that falls within some deviation from equilibrium—say, 0.0001 percent—goes up breathtakingly quickly. For our purposes, equilibrium is the state of balance that systems reach if given sufficient time and isolation to get there. For the air in the room again, equilibrium would be all the air molecules evenly distributed throughout the room. Drop an ice cube in a cup of hot tea, and the temperature of the tea and melted ice after it stabilizes is equilibrium. Recall the histograms introduced in chapter Year 4. If we were to make a histogram of the number of states, with the bins on the horizontal axis being the deviation from equilibrium (in degrees for or our melting ice in tea example), we would discover that the histogram looks like a needle if we choose bins of width, say, 0.0001 degrees. That is, essentially all the possible physical configurations of the molecules in the tea are well within 0.0001 degrees of equilibrium. If the system chooses states randomly, it will always find one in that narrow range near equilibrium. Heat can't flow from cold to hot in everyday situations because the number of particles in that ice cube, maybe a 1 with twenty-four zeroes after it, is so large that the histogram becomes so narrow that the width is too small to measure. The probability of any everyday system spontaneously walking away from equilibrium is so breathtakingly, unimaginably small that some of us are comfortable calling these things "impossible."

In a course covering thermodynamics and statistical mechanics, we use many examples to help students come to terms with this notion, but it is a challenge given our intrinsic bias against randomness and probabilistic thinking. We often start by talking about flipping coins or rolling dice. If you roll two dice, the most likely number you will roll (the *mode* of the distribution) is seven. If you roll two dice a bunch of times, seven is also the average number you get, the *mean* of the distribution. Put another way, you are averaging 3.5 for each die you roll. As a digression within our digression, it is sometimes interesting to people to notice that 3.5 is the mean number you get with each roll, but not only is it not the mode, it is not even a possible outcome of any roll of your die. In fact, if your die is perfectly designed, you expect the mode of the distribution to be all the possible outcomes: 1, 2, 3, 4, 5, and 6. If you roll a die ten times, you expect the average to be 3.50, but you are not terribly surprised if it is 3.83 or 2.96, although you might be pretty surprised if it is as high as, say, 5.11—surprised to the point of distrusting the person who provided the die. This scatter is related to the Poisson counting statistics we have been talking about, although it is not exactly the same, given the hard limits of 1 and 6 provided by the finite-faceted cube. If you now roll your die a million times, the likelihood of finding a mean even as far away from 3.50 as 3.58 is very, very, very small.

Think again of the air in a typical room. It likely has more than a billion times a billion times a billion particles, and where you find those particles in the room when you look is a "trial" akin to rolling a die. If you divide the room front to back into six even volumes, then finding one of the sections with 10 percent more particles than another section is like rolling your die more than a billion, billion, billion times and getting 10 percent more 4s than 3s. It's not gonna happen.

"Monkeys typing Shakespeare" is one of the more fun examples we calculate in class. This example is based on the oft-shared idea that enough monkeys typing randomly for sufficient duration would eventually produce all the works of Shakespeare. In class we demonstrate that this is gibberish. Using our M&M caveat that pulling one color, now typing one key, doesn't affect the next color pulled, now the next key typed, we show that if all of the monkeys that ever inhabited Earth had somehow been randomly typing one keystroke per second since the Big Bang, the probability that they would produce a single page of any work of Shakespeare is a decimal point with more than a hundred and sixty thousand zeros after it before the first nonzero digit appears. I am comfortable calling some finite number of monkeys typing any number of previously published books in any finite time impossible, just as I am comfortable saying that it is impossible that any two days or any two years afield will be identical.

A. E. Housman's poem "Stars, I have seen them fall" can be analyzed in terms of the strictly forbidden and statistically forbidden notions we have just so delightfully developed. The poem opens:

Stars, I have seen them fall,
But when they drop and die
No star is lost at all
From all the star-sown sky.

The imagery implies the statistically forbidden version of impossible, an implication that there are so many stars in the sky that when one falls and dies it is not at all possible for us to notice the loss from the stellar multitude. Here's yet another fun digression within a digression. Our Milky Way Galaxy has about two hundred billion stars, but only a few thousand are visible to us in the night sky without the optical aid of binoculars or telescopes. If too many of those few thousand started disappearing, it wouldn't take long to notice. It turns out, however, that Housman's star-falling impossibility is less statistically forbidden and more strictly forbidden, given that falling stars are not stars at all but bits of dust burning up in the atmosphere, the meteors we described earlier. So, of course, no star can be lost from the star-sown sky as a result of the incineration of dust in the atmosphere. The poem concludes:

The toil of all that be
Helps not the primal fault;
It rains into the sea,
And still the sea is salt.

Again, desalination of the oceans by freshwater rain falling into their vastness would, on the surface, appear to be a statistically forbidden task given the volume of water filling the world's oceans. Once more, however, this is an example of strictly forbidden: the freshwater rain is part of Earth's hydrologic cycle. That water was at some earlier point already part of an ocean, and it is simply cycling around and around. Earth isn't running across any meaningful new water supplies from space or spontaneously generating water in a significant quantity. The implication of the poem would then appear to be that the speaker believes that humans can do all the good works they like to try to save themselves from their fallen status to no avail. On the surface it may appear that their lack of progress on this front is due to the vastness of the problem of the depravity woven into human nature, such that all the good works of all the good people ever could barely scratch the problem's surface. Look closer, however, and you find a strictly forbidden kind of impossibility. No matter the value of good works, they simply can't fix the problem of humanity's fallen nature any more than water derived from the ocean can desalinate the ocean.

That measuring is an important part of life to me, a scientist, might not be surprising. After all, many people have come to believe that measuring represents the totality of what science is. You hear the misconception when they say, "The data collection is done. That was the science. Now the art comes in figuring out what to do with it." Indeed, learning to gather the most helpful data in the most useful way is a journey of a lifetime, but just as central—or more central—to science is the building of understanding from that data. The Henri Poincaré quotation I share with my students is "Science is no more a collection of data than a house is a pile of bricks." The pile of data has a story to tell. If we've journeyed well toward quality data collection, then that pile of data likely has many different stories it could tell, some of which we probably will miss because they are so surprising we fail to recognize them. If we've done a sufficiently good job of the teasing of narrative from our data, then we might find that some of the emergent stories will suggest the next pile of data we should gather as well as making us question other stories we have teased from other piles of data.

More than observing broadly, I really just like counting things. Maybe that's obvious from all the time we have spent looking at the beauty that issues forth from counting M&Ms or the results of rolling a die or the potential outcomes of a roomful of monkeys whapping at computer keys. Just as people can misunderstand science, they also tend to misunderstand numbers and, specifically, people who love numbers. They might see numbers as coldly robbing the narrative and beauty from the world instead of how a number opens a million possible stories, songs, and poems issuing forth. As I count, a narrative often begins to emerge, and were I fully engaged in the practice of science, I would design a set of observations to test that narrative, but typically I am not. Recently, as we are heading toward or returning from hunting and fishing adventures, Kristin and I have begun listening to pop, rock, and country songs while counting the pieces that make the structure—intro, verse 1, chorus 1, verse 2, chorus 2, bridge, chorus 3, outro—or the like. Sometimes we count the measures in each of these substructures within the songs and find patterns emerging regarding who changes things up in certain ways. We could develop a theory as to why certain songs became popular or why certain artists prefer one structure over another, but mostly we count to engage our brains during the time getting to the woods.

A different numbers game Kristin and I play as we approach a new fishing year is to ask, "If you could only use A fishing lures this year what would they be?" Here, A is a number like 3 or 5 or 10. What makes this game challenging is the disparate array of angling we do. We trout fish in streams that hold no other game fish. We scour rivers for an enormous variety of fish. We acquired a digital scale with a fish-friendly clip—the kind they use in Major League Fishing—to weigh largemouth bass at the lakes we visit, and catching "scorable" largemouth bass weighing more than one pound has become an important part of these trips, but we still like to search out crappie, perch, bluegill, and the occasional catfish. In all of these settings, the water can vary from gin clear to chocolate milk muddy. Post–cold front conditions couldn't be more different from stable high pressure. October offers a completely different fishing experience than July offers, and neither of those months is remotely like March. You get the idea just how challenging selecting five lures for the entire year would be. You're better off trying to understand how electron degeneracy has led to supernovae and the variety of chemical abundance around us. Sometimes we do a different game, pausing midyear to ask ourselves, "Suppose that going forward we could only use lures that haven't caught fish yet this year, what would we turn to?" This kind of exercise keeps the brain nimble and helps us avoid falling into ruts, reminding us of techniques that might have slipped away as we became enamored with a certain set of lures or approaches on the water.

One way I apply the above thinking to hunting is to ask myself, "If I could only hunt one property during the season ahead, what would it be and how would I approach it?" This question can be painful, as I love so many of the places we hunt, but it is a helpful exercise. The answer to the question has varied over the years, but lately, if I were confined to a single hunting locale, it almost certainly would be New Grandpa Place, the latest place to feel like home afield for me. In many ways, picking one place to hunt is like picking a small handful of lures. You can't optimize for any one species or type of hunting but need to seek generality. New

Grandpa Place defies this limitation, to a degree, as it has been the top go-to place for one type of hunting or another for me at different times. Even in the driest years, I can count on finding ducks in the always wet bottomland, and if snipe and rails are to be found anywhere, there is a good chance they will be in that New Grandpa Place marsh. For a few years, all my turkeys came from this property. But variety is there as well. The marsh yields to densely wooded bluffs that open up on top to large swaths of grass, weeds, and corn. Pheasants aren't plentiful up top, but they are present, and the DNR plants sunflowers on one section now so that it has become a reliable dove property. There are two sizable sections across the highway that I have never hunted. If I were to limit my hunting to just this property, I'd have the time and energy to explore these. Who knows what I'd find? Rarely would I be unable to locate part of the property free from other hunters.

Best of all, New Grandpa Place has become one of my two most reliable woodcock properties. It didn't start out that way. Two distinct woodcock hunting opportunities are to be found here, the sandbar willows around the marsh and the wooded edges up top. I was drawn first to the clear-cuts above where I found a population of birds that became known as Wily Woodcock. To this day, ten years later, I haven't managed to shoot one of those up-top woodcock, although I've had great success in the willows below. Let's blame it on the very steep, very long climb to the top, a climb I frequently did after busting marsh grass all morning in my waders. And the reality is that by the time I started discovering this place, I was no longer young, although, as noted earlier, at the time I utterly failed to recognize this inevitability. My first Wily Woodcock encounter came after I had swept the open fields on top in an unsuccessful attempt to raise a rooster pheasant after a morning in the marsh below. On the way up, I had passed a very small but right-age and right-density clear-cut on the uphill side of the road used by loggers and farmers, with a promising swath of berry brambles and cedars on the downhill side. The pheasant grass ran right up against this little clear-cut.

As I neared the clear-cut from the grass above, I stopped to switch chokes from modified–improved modified to cylinder–improved cylinder to spread the shot more quickly for woodcock that were likely to flush closer, and my loads from #6 lead to #7 ½, the smaller pellets providing enough knock-down power for woodcock and doing a better job of filling out the wider shot pattern. I also enjoyed a bit of leftover Halloween candy, a pheasant hunting tradition. Having made the physical and mental shift from big gaudy roosters to little russet twitterers and fortified by peanut butter cups, I headed to the clear-cut. Before I made it, a woodcock got up out of the grass on the outside edge of the woods, swinging left, not in the greatest of hurries. The gun went click, click. This wasn't the failure to fire that was to come with this gun but instead was the operator's failing to reload it after the snack and choke changing break. I'd like to say this was the only time this happened to me, but I can't. One balmy day after Thanksgiving, I parked at a lot atop the hill at Old Homestead Place, hiking the mile down through the woods to look for ducks along the creek. There is a parking lot down low, but I prefer the hike. As I neared the first hole, I went into stalk mode and got near enough that a duck flushed at fifteen yards, but you guessed it—click, click. I had walked all that way without ever loading the gun.

This first Wily Woodcock encounter should have warned me off these birds permanently. I followed up and promptly missed with both barrels as the bird flew far into a deep ravine in the mature woods. I would be back repeatedly in the coming years, always achieving similar results, miss after miss, oddity after oddity, frustration after frustration. Looking this way when a bird flushes that way. Hunkered down inspecting flora when a bird bursts out so close it's a wonder that I hadn't stepped on it. This year my woodcock success would be an almost identical repeat of the prior year's, a clean shot on a bird in the now aging clear-cut at Troutpalooza Place. Thank goodness I wasn't limiting myself to a single hunting property. Who would even consider such a thing?

YEAR 14

Driftless Safari

Let's begin this year, two years after my last successful Iowa ruffed grouse hunt, with a reflection on some of the things I miss about grouse. It's possible to make the claim that I shouldn't miss them at all because I'd had no expectation of finding them upon arriving in Iowa, making the current reality more like my imagined Iowa. But once they were part of my life, I fell into that naïve trap that so often ensnares people, expecting they would always be here (well, be here for the duration of my personal always), that tomorrow and the day after would look much like today and yesterday. If there are major themes to what you are reading, the fallacy of such thinking is one of them. Yet despite any evidence to the contrary I too am human.

One way I am human shows in a tendency to romanticize the past, such that even the most distracted reader might have noted a hint of it in these pages. One result of this observing the past through rose-colored glasses is the common claim of people that they were born too late, sometimes remarkably too late, as in Edwin Arlington Robinson's poem "Miniver Cheevy," in which we hear of "Miniver Cheevy, born too late," dreaming of "Thebes and Camelot." In Jimmy Buffett's "A Pirate Looks at Forty," the singer reflects on being born a couple hundred years too late. It seems more common, however, to over-romanticize the more recent past, feeling that one was born just a decade or two too late. I'm so certain that I've heard this discussed frequently, that we can ascribe the lazy "attributed variously" to it, although it is possible that, like so many things, "attributed imaginatively" could be more appropriate. And that's where I fall, wondering what it would have been like to arrive in my slice of heaven twenty-five years earlier. I dream of how things might have been different: my legs and grouse starting to give out near the same time, a liberal arts education remaining a more reasonable proposition to people who understood higher education to be something other than vocational training, the night sky even darker and the fields I roam even more open, Iowa existing as a purple state, a place where people would talk to each other across difference. Surely, had it been my fortune to arrive that two-and-a-half decades earlier, I would have then been pondering how glorious it must have been to be here another twenty years earlier, when the pheasant opener was still celebrated almost as a holiday, and who knows what else seemed somehow utopian. I know for certain that ducks would have been scarcer and my job challenging in different ways in the absence of our instant access to information and published papers and before the digital cameras that have been the engines driving my research project. I certainly would have missed the latest and greatest in health care, something about to play a major role in the continuation of my story.

It's fair enough to miss the grouse for the sake of seeing grouse, of knowing that the forest floor could explode without warning at any moment, providing an unnerving glimpse of beauty and wildness. The absent grouse also create a hole in my being, given their role as a link to my origin. I'll never again hunt with my dad, and although we hunted many different birds together in later years, notably pheasants, grouse will always be the bird we spent more time pursuing than all other species combined. It might be, however, that I miss grouse most for how they marked, stretched, and otherwise altered time's incessant flow. First, they extended my hunting season. Some Januaries were too snowy to hunt, but when they weren't, grouse were legal game three weeks past pheasants, adding something special to cold late January days. But more than extending seasons, they were markers of time's passage. I rarely gave them much attention early in the season, with ducks, snipe, and woodcock around, and pheasants more plentiful in the first week of the season than any other time. Grouse then became markers of the transition to late fall and early winter, a passing of the seasons. Months later, their drumming heralded the transition to real spring. I've always used many markers, beyond the habits of birds or my habits related to birds, to note the passage of time, especially winter and the transition to spring.

The mechanical characteristics of the seasons, like temperature and duration of daylight, result from Earth's coupled orbital and rotational motion. Because our orbit wraps around each year, the seasons come and go with a familiar annual cycle. The characteristics we associate with the seasons are, thus, periodic functions of time with peaks in one season and troughs in the opposite season or ascending values in one season and descending values in the opposite season. Plotting the amount of daylight (photoperiod) as a function of the day of the year yields a graph that looks a lot like a sine wave with a period of one year. It's not exactly a sine wave because of the changing speed of Earth as its distance from the Sun varies; the shape is close enough to a sinusoid that we can call it sinelike. For many characteristics of the seasons, it makes sense in my world to call the minimum of this curve midwinter and the maximum midsummer. Winter becomes the thirteen weeks centered on this minimum, and the first day of spring arrives six and a half weeks after the minimum. In practical terms, we like to talk about "slow" and "fast" parts of sinelike curves. In the slow parts, near maximum and minimum, the characteristic that is being plotted changes relatively slowly with time; in the fast parts, that same characteristic changes relatively rapidly. Winter and summer are the seasons of slow change; fall and spring are the seasons of rapid change. I like to think of the first day of spring and the first day of fall as our slipping onto the fast part of the curve as shown below.

Here's something that maybe a lot of people haven't recognized—or maybe they have but haven't celebrated it sufficiently. Late in the hunt-

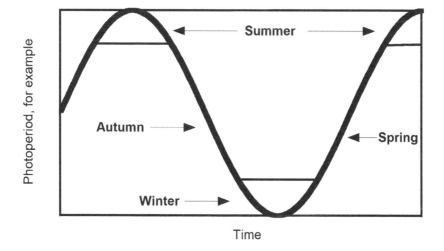

Time

ing year, when the journal has already recorded far more days afield than remain to be seized, we reach the bottom of the sinelike curve for evening daylight and start to turn back up while we are still losing morning daylight more rapidly than we are gaining it in the evening, leading to days growing shorter despite sunsets starting to creep later. My earliest sunset, when I mark evening daylight midwinter, is always about December 9. Six-and-a-half weeks later, we will have reached the "fast" part of the curve that results from graphing sunset time as a function of date, making it already evening daylight spring while still in January. You might recognize the shortest day of the year for Northern Hemisphere residents like me, photoperiod midwinter, as typically about December 21. Somewhere around January 2, we have our earliest sunrise, and all the midwinters related to daylight are past. Because Earth is massive (a bit of understatement), it is slow to respond to changes in energy input, still radiating away more heat than it receives in the north well after the solar energy input has begun increasing. We will reach our average coldest day of the year about fifteen days after we hit sunrise midwinter, thus reaching temperature midwinter. These mechanical measures of time are far more stable, if less emotionally uplifting, than bird-related measures of time. My last wood duck sighting in the fall is usually around November 1, and my first in spring around March 15. Wood duck midwinter might land halfway between these dates or squarely between sunrise midwinter and temperature midwinter. But defined as the time they are missing from the local area, wood duck winter is longer than the standard thirteen-and-a-half weeks that is a quarter of the year, suggesting the malleability of flora and fauna–based seasons.

Let's break for a moment to talk about why, during winter in the Northern Hemisphere, sunset reaches its earliest point nearly a month before sunrise reaches its latest. First, we note that the dominant factor in changing sunrise and sunset times is how the rotational axis of Earth is tilted relative to Earth's orbital axis. We have shorter days, earlier sunsets, and later sunrises in winter when our rotational axis is pointed away from the Sun. As we transition from the rotational axis pointing away from the Sun by the maximum amount possible, the daylight period starts getting gradually longer. But we need to look at the varying speed of Earth in its orbit to better understand why sunrises don't start getting earlier at the same time sunsets begin getting later.

Kepler showed that when we are closer to the Sun, we are moving faster than when we are farther away. Suppose you build a monument in the shape of an arrow that points directly at the Sun, as shown in the illustration. In the illustration, we have exaggerated how far Earth moves in its orbit in one rotation. Your monument is shown at three different times—first when Earth is directly "below" the Sun and your monument points straight up toward the top of the illustration. Next, after one rotation, your monument again points straight up but it no longer points at the Sun in this orientation. To get your monument pointed back toward the Sun, as shown by the only arrow not pointing straight up in the illustration, Earth had to rotate more than one full rotation. That is, the time from noon to

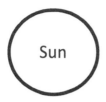

Sun

If Earth moves faster at some point in its orbit, it needs more extra rotation to return the Sun to the same point in the sky, causing the sunrise and sunset to be later than expected if the speed does not change.

Extra rotation of Earth needed to get Sun back to same location in the sky

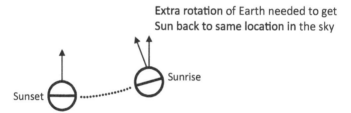

Sunset

Sunrise

Orbit

noon (or sunrise to sunrise or sunset to sunset) is longer than the time for one full rotation of Earth. We have built our clocks to correct for that extra rotation. Our clocks use twenty-four hours as the duration of a day, while Earth's rotation period is about twenty-three hours and fifty-six minutes.

If we are moving faster than average at some point in our orbit, during one rotation we will move farther along in our orbit than average. If we move farther in our orbit, then we need to rotate a little more than usual to get the Sun back directly overhead or to get from sunrise to sunrise or sunset to sunset. That is, when we are moving faster than average, the day gets to be a tiny bit longer, meaning that everything that marks a day gets a tiny bit longer—sunrise to sunrise and sunset to sunset times are both longer, forcing both sunrise and sunset to be a little later than they would be if we weren't speeding up and slowing down in our orbit. Since we are at closest approach to the Sun in early January, we are moving our fastest in orbit in December and January, so that Northern Hemisphere residents get later than expected sunsets and sunrises then, with the observed result that northerners reach the earliest sunset well before the latest sunrise each winter.

You might also note that in the illustration, when we are facing away from the Sun we call that night, and the direction we look in the sky at night varies as we move along our orbit. As a result, we have come to associate different constellations with different times of the year. Many Northern Hemisphere residents link Orion with midwinter because that is when it is high in the evening sky, say, on a clear, biting January night, when the bright stars of the familiar asterism sparkle against a sky made particularly inky by the freezing out of moisture. But rotation allows us to see a sizable fraction of the night sky from any point in our orbit, so that I enjoy watching Orion fade from view as daylight builds over the marsh while I await legal shooting time in very early October. Since we are talking about orbits and rotations, we might as well note that above Orion's head lies the constellation Auriga, and this area of the sky contains the anticenter of our Galaxy, the Milky Way. Recall our earlier discussion comparing the stars of the Milky Way to the trees of a forest. The Sun orbits the galactic center about once every 230 million years. When you are awaiting daylight over some fall marsh and you are facing Orion, watching it fade into the morning twilight, you have your back to the galactic center and are facing the outer edge of the galactic disk away from that center. While I miss grouse as a marker of time in the fall and winter woods, at least there are plenty of other ways to internalize the temporal flow, including the coming and going of woodcock.

After my Wily Woodcock failure of the previous fall, I made sure to get back up the New Grandpa Place hill earlier this next year, climbing that farm road with the clear-cut paralleling the uphill side of the road for a few hundred yards before it reaches the open fields on top, with berry brambles and mixed shrubs below. Past the clear-cut, the road makes a sharp left turn and heads for the corn, with the downhill side marked by the mature forest chasm into which the woodcock of the year prior had escaped. Where the road turns left when headed uphill, a short ledge extends right, like an arrowhead that narrows to a point within twenty yards, offering breathtaking views of the creek valley below and the ridge across the valley, while serving as evidence of how far one has climbed from the duck and snipe marsh. Walking out the arrowhead puts the berry bramble on one's right and, for a bit, the deep chasm of mature forest on the left before the chasm fades into the valley ahead. That such vexing woodcock could inhabit an abode so heavenly is one of life's enduring mysteries.

This year, I worked the clear-cut carefully, zig-zagging my way uphill from its onset. Having failed to raise a bird and wondering if the woodcock from the year before was a fluke, I opted to walk out the arrowhead to take in the view while remembering that someone's grandfather chose to make this place possible for me to enjoy at this moment. About halfway to the arrow tip, a woodcock got up no more than ten feet from me as I was lost in reverie. I'm sure I had a goofy look and glazed eyes. The bird spun left into the mature forest. I missed with both barrels as it disappeared about fifty yards out. The bird reflushed at a more respectable twenty-five yards. Bark flew from the large tree it disappeared behind as I squeezed the trigger. I followed once more, clinging precariously to the steep hillside. The bird flushed at about thirty yards and disappeared across the chasm before I could find my balance and react. Wily Woodcock, 2; this hunter, 0.

This autumn is notable for multibird days in the field. I know many hunters count on multiple birds when they go afield, but a single bird is far more typical for me. Two birds in the bag isn't uncommon, but anything more than three is pretty far out of the ordinary and worthy of note, at least if rails aren't involved. I lose a little hunger for the hunt after that first kill and don't push as hard. I gather the bird, say a little prayer of thanks, and start to appreciate other things about the day and about life, letting my focus drift a bit. I stay present enough that sometimes I will get second and third birds, but more often than not I don't.

In late September, I opened a morning of the early duck season in my little corner of Canvasback Marsh, managing a pair of blue-winged teal before stashing the decoys and kicking the pool edges. A snipe got up out in front of me, doing its cyclone spiral high into the air before turning and flying back over me at full throttle thirty yards up. I was as startled as anyone else who had been present would have been when I pulled the trigger with the bird directly over me and it folded neatly, arcing into the pool for an easy retrieve. All snipe shots are tough, but this one felt particularly good to make. After working the rest of this pool, I decided to go ahead and climb the dike to get to the next pool. When I did, another blue-winged teal erupted right in front of me, and I had a day of three teal and a snipe, a very, very big day for me. A few weeks later, I bagged a wood duck, a snipe and a blue-winged teal at New Grandpa Place. That was nearly half my annual allotment of birds in two trips.

My woodcock for the year came the very next day from Arroyo Place. I had hunted pretty hard for a second consecutive day, starting at New Grandpa Place looking for ducks. Then I went to Troutpalooza Place and worked the clear-cut that had been productive the past two years. The previous couple of years had been that perfect time when it was still dense enough to hold birds but thin enough to allow reasonable shooting. Now it seemed like maybe it was done, or if not yet finished, the end was palpable, with the sky showing more clearly through the thinning canopy. On up the hill, I found a newer, denser clear-cut that I tried to push, but the going was too hard, and it was still too young to hold much promise. The two rabbits that scrambled away from me foretold a bright future for this cut, a time when this could be a special place, as one cut aged and disappeared while the next came on, a cycle like so many other cycles. Ending the day in my arroyo, I flushed a woodcock about halfway through my push, under the buckthorn that typically held them. I had time for only one quick snap shot that didn't connect. As I approached where I thought the bird had gone in, it flushed behind a screen of brush back toward its original location, without offering any chance for a shot. I had more or less given up hope of seeing that bird again when it burst off the ground and curled high into the treetops. I missed once more with the first trigger pull, but managed a second shot, yielding another one of those times where you don't actually see the bird go down, but you don't see it fly off, and something about the silence tells you it is likely hit and down. I scrambled through the scree of the arroyo and up the other bank to find my woodcock, wings splayed, resting atop the vegetation. My journal says, "It was a joyous, sad moment." Often, my journal has cryptic phrases and notes that I can't quite decipher the meaning of years later. I think I will remember what I was calling this clump of trees or that lure, but I don't. I am not certain why this particular bird in the hand was any more joyous or sad than any other bird, since they all produce a mix of those feelings. Perhaps, it was something about the length of the chase and the multiple reflushes or the way the bird was displayed.

I popped into the prairie grass for the walk back to the parking area, where I found a woman and a young girl. They were engaged in something called Driftless Safari. Posts had been placed around various wild areas and atop these posts were embossed plates that could be rubbed over with a pencil to transfer the image to a guidebook to commemorate having located the spot. As noted previously, not everyone is excited to see a hunter come out of the woods, particularly after there has been shooting in the vicinity, but this pair asked whether I'd gotten anything. When I answered in the affirmative, they wondered if they could see the bird. I am always pleased when a bird is not too damaged by shot, but as I held my woodcock out for them to admire, likely the first they'd ever seen, I was particularly pleased this bird was little damaged. They seemed genuinely appreciative of the opportunity to get something out of their Driftless Safari beyond a rubbing of an emblem on a post.

YEAR 15

The Lake

The idea of a histogram was introduced in chapter Year 6. One histogram showed that most of the woodcock I have taken and eventually eaten have been brought to hand from about October 18 to November 2. The weekend just before or encompassing Halloween has been the most productive time. My woodcock success has spanned autumn, stretching from the very beginning of the season to the last day, suggesting that it's sensible for me to hunt the entire season, early to late, instead of merely pursuing the twittering brown bird with the beguiling eyes only on the few days on either side of Halloween, but if I can only afford to leave work early for a last-hour hunt a few days a year, it is wise to stack those stolen hours right around Halloween. The second most common time for woodcock success would be ten or so days earlier, during our fall break. I don't know what the students think of fall break, but it comes just in time for me, as I am slipping sufficiently behind in my work, that I need that time to get back on top of things. I've always been a morning person, arising about 4:00 am, whether I want to or not. My brain says, "Hey, it's day. Let's go. There are things that could be done." So when fall break arrives, hunting a few hours in the morning still leaves plenty of day to get closer to caught up on work.

This year is the next and final year in the twenty-two-year journey recounted in these pages without a woodcock bagged. This can be traced, in part, to my decision to give up the usual fall break activities to make a second lake trip of the year with my parents. Sure, a couple of woodcock hunting mornings were lost, but the missing catch-up time had a greater impact on me, leading to a need for "catch-up catch-up" on my return. This catching up on catch up was made more difficult when typical midsemester fatigue was compounded by a quick-turnaround trip. The drive from Iowa to The Lake was always a relatively grueling but interesting affair, taking a full eleven or twelve hours, with a long stretch of two-lane road that felt more like driving back through time than winding through space. The yard signs displaying hand-scrawled messages exhorting passersby to consider "Smith for Sheriff" made one wonder if Smith had run for sheriff any time in the past fifty years. Decades after I last saw the practice anywhere else, one town always had people with fried chicken buckets attempting to extract cash from motorists trapped by the lone stoplight on the highway through town. Once, a would-be collector held a cardboard sign (hand-scrawled like a Smith for Sheriff sign, obviously) that read, "Help, the orphans!" As I sped south out of town, I kept my eyes locked on the rearview mirror, worried that some sort of orphan zombie horde might be gaining on me.

My parents' first trip to The Lake, at the invitation of friends, was eleven months before I was born. In those days the resort (more of a semirustic fishing camp than a resort by contemporary standards) was so active that if one didn't jump on an open slot or if one gave up the annual weeklong reservation, then it would likely be years before the opportunity reappeared. Fishing resorts, as well as attitudes toward recreation and leisure time, evolve as surely as do woodcock covers and morel trees. Years later, the place had fallen into disuse and disrepair, the result of shifting attitudes toward what constituted a meaningful family vacation. An aging resort owner who had always been something of a steely-edged challenge contributed to the issue. He grew ever tougher to work for and live with, so that even the hardest working employees couldn't measure up and were driven away. One year, on the last day of our visit, when the only paying guests were my relatives, and even that number had dwindled, we all grabbed mowers and trimmers, working over the grounds to make them somewhat presentable.

One of the friends who first invited my family to The Lake lives on in our fishing in multiple ways. The technique of pointing the bow of a boat toward the bank, creating a significant fishing challenge for the angler in the rear seat, was so perfected by this person that we describe the action as a verb built from his name, a verb Kristin and I still use when our boat gets turned perpendicular to whatever cover we are fishing. This friend also owned a small lure-making shop in a converted garage, topwater prop plugs slowly emerging from blocks of wood turned on a simple lathe, before receiving a coat of paint from an airbrush and having the hooks and props screwed in by hand. In the days before everything came blister-packed from somewhere else, these lures could be slipped into cardboard boxes and distributed regionally. It was the kind of operation that wasn't going to earn anybody a living but made perfect sense back when we still manufactured things instead of relying on imports. You know, making a product the world wants or needs—diesel engines in this case—all week for a living and then use the skills you've spent a lifetime honing to build things you want and love on the weekend, modest yet beautiful bass lures in this case. Slightly embarrassed, my mom often related the story of how ashamed she was as a youngster when she had to take sandwiches made on delicious homemade bread because they couldn't afford the newfangled presliced bread everyone thought was the greatest thing. That pretty much captures how I feel about these lures looking back. In my younger days, these hand-made plugs seemed hopelessly old-fashioned and inferior to the latest injected-molded plastic creations being produced by Bomber, Norman, or Rebel. Thus, the world erodes.

I spent a few Saturday mornings watching the lures come to life while my dad helped some with the process, taking payment in the form of lures, so that today I have a box full of antique topwater prop plugs, collector's items no doubt, but I have more interest in collecting experiences that make clear the connections we have across time and space. So these irreplaceable beauties remain in my regular bass fishing lineup. Nothing in the world compares to the moment a chug-chug retrieve is paused and a heavy bass rolls on a lure with so much history.

Our fall break excursion represents the only time we ever went to The Lake twice in a year and my first look at the place at a time other than very near the first of June. It was now a long drive for me. We had been able to continue these annual treks for the few years since my parents' Iowa visits ended because their drive to The Lake was much shorter and more straightforward than my winding route past hand-painted signs. While the week at The Lake was certainly not easy on anybody, it lacked the hip and knee pounding of rough terrain hunting. In June of this year, however, observing both my parents made it clear to me that we were nearing an end here too. Even the shorter drive was taking a serious toll on my mom. While my approach to angling had always been go, go, go and try this and that and move, move, move, flowing with whatever the day brought, my dad had been a cautious planner, doing things precisely and exactly, never deviating from the blueprint of the day. That blueprint was the same as the blueprint of the day before and the year before. If I dumped my tackle box in a rush to change lures, it wasn't a shock, but when my dad turned over his box or kept forgetting to unclip the boat's kill switch before standing up or stepped on his rod or drove off with the flashlight on the bumper of the truck, it was so out of character that it felt like Earth had shifted on its axis. Believing that the next June would be a 50/50 proposition at best, I organized the October trip as a potential last look at the place that had been so much a part of our lives. Indeed, it was our final time sharing that magic, now just a memory receding into the ever-more-distant horizon.

Time belongs to a class of particularly fascinating mysteries that consist of commonplace ideas that we are all sure we understand, at least until we try to articulate that understanding in a meaningful definition of the concept. An understanding of what time is has proven elusive, leading some physicists and philosophers to suggest that maybe it doesn't exist, that it is merely an illusion related to how we perceive the universe. It's an idea that bubbles up and disappears, only to reappear years or decades later, into the vacuum created by our missing theory of time. Nearly a quarter of a century ago, Julian Barbour wrote *The End of Time: The Next Revolution in Physics*. In 2018 Carlo Rovelli wrote *The Order of Time*. In each of these works, the author suggests that reality is something like a series of "nows" that exist in a network. Rather than time flowing from past to future, "the past" is simply those "nows" we have experienced by being at the particular network nodes that contained them. Our being at those network nodes allows us to form memories of them, creating a sensation of not only a past but also a future that contains "nows" we are yet to experience. Although this simple picture doesn't do justice to the theories posited in either book, it does provide us with a framework to imagine different possibilities for what we mean when we discuss the flow of time. This framework has made appearances in literature over the years. In *The Road to Tinkhamtown*, Corey Ford's classic hunting story first published in 1969, we find these ideas, as characters argue about what "the past" is and whether it still exists someplace that we have simply moved on from.

Five decades at The Lake, one week at a time turning "nows" into "the past," is at least as good as fall hunting for tracking the "same but different" character of life's flow, be it in disappearing patronage at the resort, evolution of the resort's physical structures and ownership, the way we approached fishing, or the fish population itself. From the early, thriving days of the resort, when guests could play bingo and square dance in addition to fish, central to my memory is the wooden dock that was accessed via a metal grate walkway and that housed a machine that dispensed small glass bottles of Coca-Cola for a dime, the classic red machine adorned with white script letters. There, I used crickets to pull bass and bluegill from the shade the structure provided, eventually learning that bluegill after bluegill could be snagged from under the middle of the dock by sneaking a cricket through the crack between adjacent sections. The trick, then, was to gently work the bluegill sideways so that it could fit up through the crack. As the years flowed by, crickets were replaced by jigs and small spinners that occasionally produced something surprising, like a skipjack. Some years, the water was so high that it covered the walkway to this ancient dock and spread over rocks and walls around the resort, flooding the pool with water people chose not to swim in. Often these floods scattered the bass or made them leery if the tide had turned and the level was headed back to normal, leading to tough angling for those in boats, but the fishing around the resort was never better.

At some point, exactly when is lost in the haze of the past, the wooden deck of the dock was replaced by smoother, longer-lasting concrete atop the foam floats. This dock became a secondary boat mooring area after a new covered facility was built around the other side of the resort. The cover did its job of keeping out the rain but wasn't the panacea my dad had imagined over all the years of pumping out the boat after a rain, years of complaining, however mildly, about this resort falling further behind the times, one of the last without a place to store the boat under cover. The birds that sought shelter under the cover brought their own issues.

The fish cleaning station moved to the new covered dock, the turtles moving with it, individual turtles that had been resident there since well before we knew of The Lake. In the early days, we would arise at 4:00 each morning and be fishing by 5:00. Following a huge breakfast after a morning of casting, we would take my mother out to troll near midday. An evening of casting would follow. In the later years, when the wear and tear of a life of casting, chain sawing, and mowing had worn out my dad's shoulder, the evening casting was replaced by a second round of trolling. Early on, the limited trolling with small clothespin style spinnerbaits was for white bass, but the angling was really all about largemouth bass, and largemouth bass fishing was all about slow crawling Texas-rigged plastic worms through the red rocks. We kept and ate those bass too, feeding the carcasses to the grateful turtles living under the cleaning station, until the "Don't kill your catch" movement from the Bass Angler Sportsman Society swept the nation, after which we only kept white bass, sauger, and the occasional catfish. Trolling became more important for filling the freezer for winter, and we did this fishing with crankbaits that produced an array of fish species far broader than the spinners ever had. My mom never bought into the new paradigm, disgusted when her trolling resulted in a five-pound largemouth bass instead of a skinny ten-inch white bass she could eat. After we discovered crankbaits, hard plastics came to rule our casting as well, as they caught largemouth and smallmouth bass quite well but were particularly effective on sauger, the pinnacle of fish for the freezer. Sauger in the lake became like grouse in our woods. The last eight years of casting and trolling produced not a single sauger bite. White bass were the ultimate "Who knows what this year will bring?" species.

Some years, we never found them at all. Other years, schools would roam a large flat, eight to ten feet deep, where a flooded creek arm met a flooded river. Trolling that flat would turn them up, the school always on the roam across the flat, us trying to stay in contact with the school, our paths intersecting sufficiently often to make it worth the effort. Some years, the white bass would drive schools of shad to the surface as they do more commonly later in the year, after our traditional June week. When the surface churned with life-and-death activity, drawing in birds as if we were adrift on the ocean somewhere, we could cast heavy lures into the crashing school, catching fish cast after cast as long as we could see them. They'd disappear and then reappear sometime later, a quarter of a mile or more away. We'd fire up and go after them. One of my fondest memories of my dad's father comes from a white bass year shortly before my grandparents became unable to travel to The Lake, which itself was shortly before my grandfather passed away. Some years, I fished from my grandfather's boat for morning and evening casting, while my dad fished with his brother. During this last year of such an arrangement, we would end each morning chasing schools of white bass around, my grandfather exhorting me to use my younger eyes to find them crashing the surface in the distance while he waited to get on the throttle. Such is the intensity of a white bass feeding frenzy that it was possible to get carried away. One story we remember is of the father and son team of a family that visited The Lake with us for a few years near the middle of our run there. The son, ten or twelve years old, reared back to make a long two-handed cast into the mayhem, inadvertently driving the treble hook of the heavy tail spinner into his dad's ear as he did so. When his dad brought this infraction to his attention, he threw the rod to the floor of the boat, grabbed another, and hurriedly started casting with it.

One thing remained as constant as the turtles by the fish-cleaning station. For the last thirty years of our annual angling rite, my dad and I would start every morning casting the same point, which always produced fish, usually black bass but the occasional white bass or wipers (white bass–striped bass hybrids), and routinely sauger early on. We could pick our way across The Lake in the dark, knowing by heart the location of every hidden navigation buoy to avoid on our way to this point, the last one before the smaller river dumped into the main channel of the large river that was dammed to make this huge reservoir. A flat shelf no more than five feet deep spread for probably three hundred acres off this point. Given sufficient patience, one could drift around this flat to find scattered saugers. But first light always brought us to the point where we tossed crankbaits right up next to the rusty dirt and gravel, the lips of the diving lures ricocheting through the rock field. Rare was the day we hadn't boated a nice fish or two or six by 5:30. Amid so many memories from so many sunrises there, a few mornings stand out clearly.

On the first of these memorable mornings, we had a school of bass pinned against the shore. I was doing particularly well catching fat largemouth in the two- to four-pound range on my go-to lure of that era—an original Bagley's Small Fry Shad. I've read that these original Bagley's are so valuable as fish catchers that they are highly sought after, fetching top dollar even used. One of my extra tackle boxes is crammed full of them in all sorts of models, colors, and conditions. Kristin looks a bit askance in my direction when I still throw one once in a while, much as I do with those topwater spinners my dad helped make, returning to a past that may or may not still exist somehow. There must have been a local bass club holding a tournament that launched at 6:00, because about 6:15, three boats raced in and stopped directly behind us. To their credit they did not try to push us off or cast around us, even if they did crowd us slightly, making sure their desires were known. For my part, I was unduly cruel, admiring each bass a skosh longer than necessary before slipping it back over the gunwale. I probably caught eight bass for a total weight of twenty-five pounds over a twenty-minute span while they were watching.

Many years later, a different school of largemouth, maybe (likely?) direct descendants of the bass in that earlier school, had a school of shad pinned against the bank of the point. This frenzy didn't last a quarter of the time of that earlier feed, but it was more chaotic, with shad flying out of the water and bass hammering our lures with shoulder-wrenching thunder on every cast. By this time, the crankbait was a crawdad-colored plastic-rattling Shad Rap, never quite the bass producer the Small Fry Shad had been, but better, much better, on other species. A great blue heron made this morning particularly special, The Lake's having evolved to be full of the leggy birds. When we would pull up to a point, they would fly off, squawking their disapproval. If one were particularly interested in keeping its territory, we could ease within a hundred yards or so before it reluctantly departed. On this morning, however, the heron stayed locked right there, no more than a medium-distance crankbait cast away, unable to pull itself from the shad bonanza. The bass had pushed those baitfish hard against the feet of the waiting heron, causing the bird to do something I had never seen before and have never seen since. In fact, I asked my ornithologist friend, with whom I regularly discussed bird observations, about it, and he had never heard of such behavior being documented, even though his life had been fully committed to studying bird behavior of all sorts. You see, the fishing was so good that the heron couldn't eat fast enough, and it was tossing shad onto the rocks behind it, caching those fish for later.

Each morning after ninety minutes, give or take, at our most favored point, we would explore other points, each with special stories from the past—the little point, sheep's ridge, the little bay, light pole point, the point east of light pole. In later years, I could convince my dad, with sufficient prodding, to end the morning casting one of the several offshore areas we trolled. Our final morning of rapid-fire bass catching at The Lake came at one of these structures, the white bass flat where a flooded creek entered a flooded river. The locals call these flats "ledges" on this particular impoundment in the mid-South. Nowadays, everyone else calls these ledges as well, given how readily information is available—if not the understanding that comes from acquiring that information slowly over a lifetime. The Lake was down a couple of feet this year, placing this particular ledge nearer the surface, where I could dig down to the bottom with one of the crankbaits I preferred, a size smaller and a lot more orange than the locals prefer. We positioned ourselves so that the wind would blow us across the flat and we could fan casts in all directions as we drifted by. My dad struggled, his aging joints and muscles making him unable to cast as far as needed to cover the area, cranking the lure down cast after cast. It was the type of rapid-fire angling I was built for, and I managed to catch eleven three- to five-pound bass in our first three drifts across the flat before the fish shut off or we lost track of them. To this day, it remains one of the most productive half hours of fishing of my life.

The fishing on our fall trip was remarkably different from what we'd experienced in June. Pro anglers talk all the time about the challenge of fishing these southern impoundments in the fall, when the baitfish scatter and push shallow, far back up creek channels. Indeed, shad swarmed the bay of the resort, in a way my brain couldn't have imagined no matter how much I read about the phenomenon. In his 1999 book, *Ice Finders: How a Poet, Professor and Politician Discovered the Ice Age*, Edmund Blair Bolles writes of how important it was to see vast sheets of ice covering Earth horizon to horizon before the mind could truly come to terms with a concept so monumental, so absurd as the Ice Age, when sheets of ice covered so much of the Northern Hemisphere. That's how those shad were for me, to some degree. I caught a few nice bass, including a couple on plastic swimbaits, from the same ledge that produced the three spectacular drifts a year and a half earlier, but the angling was slower than we were accustomed to, and something felt amiss given that none of the bass came from our special point. Even though this trip wasn't primarily about the fishing,

I am glad I had the opportunity to experience The Lake when it was so different from what I knew, serving as a reminder that how we envision reality is too often built primarily or entirely on our personal experience, which is too narrow to provide a full, unbiased picture. This lake is not the same place in October as it is in June, just as surely as it is not the same lake and I am not the same person we were when we first met all those decades ago. Surely, if ever a reason existed to fail to bag a woodcock some autumn, the honing of this recognition is such a reason.

A couple weeks after the lake experience, on November second, I found myself climbing the hill at New Grandpa Place. I quartered through the little clear-cut, making sure to push out to the prairie grass edge periodically. Nearly to the end of the cut, a brown rocket exploded, hard and low, as fast as a woodcock can go, seemingly headed for the next county or the next state or the Gulf. I never caught up, missing well behind the bird before it disappeared into the chasm of mature forest. To my surprise, it was there when I followed up, springing off the ground with the same authority it had earlier, and I failed to catch up yet again, feeling my accumulating years, slow and sluggish.

Deciding to push the clear-cut once more as I headed back downhill, I got a more traditional, loftier flush as the bird rose nearly straight up before heading out toward the road, providing me a great look. Still, I whiffed with both barrels as the woodcock cleared the berry brambles and disappeared down the hill below them. Clearly, the birds in this covert were in my head. These were to be the only woodcock flushes of my fall. Wily Woodcock, 3; this hunter, 0.

YEAR 16

Woodcock Throughout the Year

We could have begun discussing spring woodcock a couple of years earlier, but I have saved them for now, the third consecutive year we witnessed a male woodcock mating display at Arroyo Place. I have friends who know woodcock only through this so-called sky dance. So spectacular is it that Greg Hoch titled his book on the life history of the woodcock *Sky Dance of the Woodcock*. That text devotes more than three full pages to quotations from no fewer than nineteen authors attempting to describe this annual ritual. Each of these efforts to capture the essence of the event is somehow accurate but limited. Taken in their entirety, they paint a delightful picture that would seem adequate until you actually witness a male bird—or better yet, several birds—giving it a go. Only then does one recognize why a person might deem any nineteen descriptions of the sky dance insufficient, feeling obliged to add to that list. Hoch offered the best advice: "STOP! If it is springtime and you live in an area that has woodcock habitat, don't read anymore. Spend a few evenings outside listening for yourself. Record your own impressions of the sky dance."

I shall not try to match the fuller, more poetic descriptions given elsewhere, only noting that the male bird creates a series of buzzing calls, peents, not unlike the buzz of a nighthawk, on the ground before taking flight in a soaring spiral that carries the bird to the limits of sight in the gloaming and ends with a fluttering tumble back to earth. A few times, Kristin and I have been very close to the unfolding action. The fish stocking road that leads into Arroyo Place, crossing the arroyo and paralleling the stream to the back edge of the public land, has been a particularly good place to catch woodcock in spring. Once, while the bird was in the air, we managed to move into the arroyo where we could watch the performer as he peented in the middle of the road before launching into that high spiral. He would lift off the ground in a little jump with each raspy peent, turning slightly so that his next peent was aimed in a different direction, eventually covering a full rotation with his peents. After flight, he landed in what appeared to us to be the exact same spot for the next merry-go-round of peent-ing. A year earlier, I had stood in the middle of the same road mere feet from where a bird was peenting when it was too dark to see him on the ground or in the air, but I could hear that liquidy gurgle as he fluttered back to earth, each landing carrying him directly over me, so close I could feel the displaced air from his flight swirl around my head. I can only assume he knew I was standing there, but I did wonder how I would explain it in the emergency room—woodcock protruding from the back of my head, long beak impaled there, both of us em-barrassed. Years earlier, at Old Homestead Place, I was moving grassy cover away from the trail edge with a walking stick while my dad and I were hunting morels. I called out, "Hey, look. It's a bird wing. No, it's a dead bird. No, it's a woodcock hen on a nest." She let me retract the grassy sheath from over her nest and gently slip it back into place without budging. There must have been sky dancing there that year, and Kristin and I have stopped by Old Homestead Place occasionally to listen for peenting but have heard none.

A different kind of interesting woodcock encounter occurred for Kristin and me in June as we were heading north to Wisconsin to fish and hike, as we do at least once or twice a summer. I know. I know. In a story with so much focus on woodcock hunting, we should be going toward Lake Superior to hunt instead of fish, but the academic calendar is what it is, making summer trips more manageable. While others dream of retiring south to warmth, we dream of the big lake with grouse and woodcock woods spreading widely from the southern shore.

We frequent one particular lake because it is isolated and ideal for our float tubes—our favorite summer fishing method. The lake produces small bass aplenty, but it is hard fighting, eye-poppingly large bluegill that represent the main attraction. If time is short or we have a long drive ahead or things are a little cold, we will edge along the lake on land, sliding in toward the shore for casts between the standing rushes. Much of the wooded shore is swampy, and we regularly flush half a dozen woodcock in an hour or two of fishing. However we approach it, this lake has become one of our prime lakes of summer.

This business of fishing in float tubes is something I have done for a very long time, and it would be interesting to give hunting in a tube a try but I'm not sure I could make it work, given my history with the devices. Even though the tubes were always very clearly stamped "For use only in still water," we never actually used them in lakes when I was young, instead exploring all manner of rivers, creeks, streams, and trickles flowing through the country that had raised generations of my family. The fishing was generally sublime. I've had days of catching more than two hundred fish, days with dozens and dozens of heavy smallmouth bass, a day that produced a four-pound largemouth bass from water so thin you would have sworn a lamprey couldn't fit, a day when a twenty pound carp towed me around the river, days and days of fish to fill a lifetime with memories.

The encounters weren't always with fish. One day, I drifted past a hen ruffed grouse that had brought her brood to the edge of the minuscule creek to dust and preen. Most of the trips from my younger days were with the friend who was eating peanuts when quail buzzed us at Grandpa Place. The two of us were drifting through a fast stretch of water that was too deep to use our feet to slow us on the bottom. We paid close attention in these instances because, when it suddenly was shallow enough, one could lose a fair amount of skin from a combination of tube velocity and rocky bottom. I looked up from assessing the potential for impending bottom contact to see a snake coming at

me hard. I am certain the snake was not poisonous—people claimed we had cottonmouths in our waters, but I'd been in those waters aplenty, practically living my summers in and around them, without ever seeing evidence of one—and meant me no harm, simply looking to catch a ride on what it thought was a log floating past. I was none too keen on the idea. It took a ridiculous amount of whacking the water's surface with my rod tip (I have broken more $100+ rods in more odd ways than you can likely imagine, but that's a series of stories for another place and time) to convince the snake that this was not a log suitable for basking on.

On a different float through the Hoosier National Forest, we miscalculated the nature of the water. It was slow to the point of near stagnation and full of sticks that slashed at our legs. The fishing for crappies in those sticks wasn't bad, but the going was beyond tough. At one point I reached forward to pull a limb back so I could slip around to the left of it. I had no idea my hand had pinned a sunning snake to that limb until I pulled its surprised head within a foot or so of my surprised head. Etched in my mind is the scene of the miraculous flying snake after my sudden release of the limb under tension.

Once, after I'd already moved to California, I flew back for a summer visit to the streams of Indiana. In those days it wasn't rare for me to work a forty-hour shift as a graduate student. These usually occurred because I was deep into some mystery in the lab, curious about what would turn up next, and before I realized what had happened, it was the next day. Prior to this trip, however, we had some deadline for a paper or a proposal that had kept me busy all night and through the next day before departing Oakland on a 10 pm flight that would lead to a connection in Chicago about 6 am local time. Nowadays, I wouldn't be surprised to fall asleep in my desk chair between classes, but in those days I absolutely couldn't sleep sitting up, no matter my level of fatigue. So I spent the overnight flight reading and watching the stars out the window. My parents met me at the Indianapolis airport, and we ate at a chain restaurant famous for its breakfasts, me downing the kind of heavy meal that would knock me right asleep today, no matter how much I'd already slept. When we pulled into my parents' driveway, I'd been awake about fifty hours, and there was my childhood friend, canoe loaded, ready for a day of adventure on the water. Really, what choice did I have? It was a lovely day of fishing, but I might have managed to doze a bit while sitting that day.

Later in the trip, I was back floating stagnant water in a tube. At a break I found a leech firmly attached to my ankle. All was fine until the flight back to California, when the attachment site grew itchy, red, and so swollen I had to remove my shoe. This reaction was sufficient to prompt me to see a physician at the university health clinic, a poor urban doctor who likely didn't understand things like creek tubing and woodcock. She kept asking, "You're sure it wasn't a tick?" "No, it wasn't a tick. Hey, did I tell you about the day I caught the biggest largemouth bass of my life, the day I had seventy-six ticks on me?"

Without a doubt, the most dangerous animal I ever encountered while tubing was myself. Given the conditions we fished, the tubes were prone to sudden, catastrophic failure, usually the result of suspect decision making. Twice, I've had the tube hook on fallen trees as I was going by and pop, leading to the need to pull myself along the trunk until I reached shore to find a farmer's field that led to a road and a long walk back to the truck, dragging the plastic ruins of a tube behind me. Never is such a journey without nettles, so many nettles. Once, my childhood friend and I were floating a small creek and getting weary after a long day of fish after fish. The creek had carved a deep channel that made it impossible to tell where one was, steep muddy banks comprising most of the majestic view that day. At one point, the bank seemed navigable, so I decided to clamber up to get a read on how much farther we had to the take-out bridge. That one should remove one's tube before attempting to scale a nearly vertical mud slick is so obvious that it hardly needs mentioning. My only defense is that it had been a day of hard travel under a blazing Indiana sun. I fell down that incline with a mighty thump, the tube making a nice air bag to cushion my landing, at least until it popped. We walked out a long field drainage ditch that landed us on the highway by a tiny house with tar paper siding, the house I knew as the one my parents first lived in when they were married. I thought of days afloat like these and smiled politely when I was at some awards dinner as a senior in college, and a physics faculty member I knew marginally asked what I did for fun besides work in the lab all night of course. "Fish," I responded, not always telling people that I hunted as well. "Ahh," he replied, "I might take up fishing some day when I'm older and need a more sedentary activity to fill my time."

Back in the current year and our drive north to our tubing lake, we visited a state park in Minnesota to fish a particularly interesting stretch of river by walking the rocky shore. We'd had a great evening of fishing and were winding out of the park on the narrow road in full darkness, listening to, of all things, a recap of the NHL draft that day. God bless satellite radio. As we rounded a curve, a small bird fluttered off the road edge and disappeared into the unilluminated forest, causing us to look at each other and ask, "Was that a woodcock in the headlights?" When the second curled out just a minute or two later, we were fairly sure. By the time the headlights caught the escape of the eleventh one, no doubt remained that these were woodcock. Maybe this is a ho-hum every night experience for those of you who don't live in Iowa. I've no idea, but it was so special for us that we have intended to attempt to replicate the experience but haven't made it yet.

When fall rolled around, it was a season of New Grandpa Place demonstrating why it had supplanted Old Homestead Place as my special half section that feels like coming home. All my ducks came from there, including a rare three-bird daily limit of stunning drake woodies. Up top, there was a clear-cut that was much larger than the Wily Woodcock clear-cut and bordered by what appeared to my eye to be a more interesting mix of mature trees. It was a bit older than the Wily Woodcock cut but looked to be young enough for woodcock use. I simply never found a bird there, not one, even when grouse were still in play. One morning this year, after a duck hunt, I worked through this cut to where it emptied into the mouth of a deep, ragged draw leading back down to the valley floor. The mouth that separated the draw from the farm fields above had a gentle dishpan shape with a few fruit trees and remnant plants that surely were once cultivated flowers, long ago naturalized. Someone, New Grandpa perhaps, had lived here. The place had returned so thoroughly to wild that it perhaps had been home to New Great-Grandpa or even New Great-Great-Grandpa.

Often, I rested in this spot, leaning against an oak tree, watching squirrels come and go. Today as I rested, I heard the unmistakable rustle made by a flock of turkeys moving through dry leaves in the bottom of the draw. They were headed my way, protected from view by the steep sides of the minivalley. Stripping myself of orange vest and hat, I crawled closer to the lip of the draw but could catch no sight of the birds, so I slipped back against a small tree and waited to see what would happen. What happened was a turkey head on the end of a long neck periscoping up over the lip a mere thirty feet in front of me. I have some rules that I break so frequently that it's almost embarrassing to call them rules. One of them is to never shoot a turkey when the body of the bird is not visible, but this bird, craning its neck (turkeying its neck?), was doing everything possible to make the target zone of head and neck clear. So there I was, once again shooting a turkey with a cylinder choke and 7 ½ shot. Chaos followed the shot, birds scattering everywhere. My bird vanished, making it impossible to know with certainty the outcome of the shot. One bird scrambled up the far bank, not more than twenty-five yards distant, conceivably the bird I had tried to shoot. I settled the gun on its head, planning to either complete the unfinished business with my bird or fill my second tag in a single day. The improved cylinder barrel went click. Fortunately, the first bird was lying dead among the large rocks at the bottom of the crevice.

It was also to be the year I got my first woodcock at New Grandpa Place, but it was not one of the Wily Woodcock. I visited their lair twice and never bumped a bird. We won't count this in the score sheet, although we probably should; one must suspect they were there, wily enough to let me walk by them more than once without a peep.

This was the year that I recognized that the sandbar willows in the marsh land below held birds more regularly than did the clear-cuts above. My first woodcock encounter came while I was working the perimeter of the main pool, trying to get a snipe airborne. Exhausted from unsure footing in the boot-sucking muck, I wobbled up into the willows for firmer ground to rest on, and a woodcock erupted within a few feet of me. Startled and weary, I didn't even try to get the gun to my shoulder. The bird offered a shot on the reflush, but still flustered, I fumbled with the gun's safety until the bird was long gone.

A week later, I made what felt like a major eureka discovery, a surprise that had been lurking just outside the headlight beams. I don't ever see others hunting ducks there because, at least in part, the trailless way in is full of tangles and the occasional swampy mire. To get into place takes me about twenty minutes of tiring, disorienting struggle in complete darkness, the last major hurdle being a water-filled ditch to cross, a soft-bottomed channel that can reach right to the top of the waders. After that ditch I need to decide how close I can work to the pool for the first round of pass shooting before I kick the edges or sit and decoy with the paltry four or five decoys I can lug in. The closer I get to the pool, the better the shots will be, but the more likely I will bust the birds too early. Whatever I decide, the goal is to be in place twenty minutes before legal shooting, ready to listen to the marsh awaken to greet the morning while my legs recover from the slog. I'm listening for telltale sounds of other species of ducks among the raucous wood ducks, and my ears are always attuned to the "scaip" of snipe starting the day. The ducks start flying early as I hope against hope that my labor to get to just the right spot at just the right time hasn't been for nil with all the ducks departing before legal shooting light. When the crows disperse, it typically marks the end of the first flight of ducks and time for me to plan my next move.

On this morning, a week after first encountering the down-low New Grandpa Place woodcock, I was gliding through the routine. At one point, three teal circled the pool in front of me and disappeared out over the creek. My first thought a moment later was "Oh, one has peeled off and is coming back to land." Soon it was evident this was no duck descending from the heights. I wish I had a picture of my face the moment I first realized it was a woodcock and it was going to settle into the willows. Was this new behavior or had I been so marsh bird–focused all these years that I missed woodcock landings? Since that first one, I see them fly in regularly. Where are they coming from when they drop in from such a height? Did they overnight on the ridgetop and head to the mucky lowland for breakfast? Or could these actually be flight birds that have traveled all night to find my little slice of paradise? Or is it something completely different? All I know now is that in addition to watching and listening for ducks and snipe, I am ready to glimpse woodcock heading in. Having bagged my first New Grandpa Place woodcock in the willows that morning, I hunt those willows with regularity, whether I've seen birds descend or not.

YEAR 17
Finding What You Seek

I have the soul of a generalist, interested in wandering forest and field, allowing my senses to meld into the wild, letting the universe tell me what should be my focus that day, rather than imposing my will on the universe. It shows in my project built on taking repetitive images year after year of the small patch of sky (recall it's the size of your one-quarter of your fingernail held at arm's length) every clear night from late February through early October. That kind of repetition allows us to see things—rare or subtle—that would be missed taking better images with multimillion-dollar equipment on a mountaintop once a year. This approach to research is akin to my hunting approach—allowing the universe to identify a focus, which results in multiple projects in disparate areas spinning off.

Sitting in one spot and letting the universe come to you, seeing what you notice as the universe talks to you, is not the way science typically gets done these days. Usually one needs a laser focus on a very specific target. That's a very good approach, a necessary approach, but not the only approach. It's possible to miss things that way, as if you were walking at night with a headlamp that allows you to see very clearly what is in the beam and virtually nothing outside it, only turning your head to shine your light where you expect it to illuminate the most meaningful thing in your path. It's a good way to walk but not the only way, just as hunting birds with dogs is a good way to hunt, just not the only way. As I walk to work in the dark each morning, I will meet people out walking for exercise with their headlamps illuminating the road directly in front of them. They must mistrust me out there walking in the dark, but I see pretty well, my eyes adapted to what I'm doing, as long as I can avoid their beams. The possibility of confirmation bias can creep in too, when we allow an observation to confirm our model despite the observation being insufficiently broad to provide that support. For example, it is often said that a "full Moon madness" afflicts people, leading to a sharp increase in trauma-related emergency room visits during a full Moon. Many studies, carried out by people who know their statistics well enough to understand that monkeys aren't going to type Shakespeare, have shown no increase in such emergency room visits during a full Moon, even though you might expect a tiny increase since people might be more likely to be outside at night during the full Moon given that moonlight lets one see to do things like angling for catfish. Still, emergency room visits are subject to the vagaries of sampling and counting statistics, so some nights will be busier than others, just randomly. When one of these occurs near a full Moon, we are likely to use that as evidence to support our "full Moon madness" theory, conveniently forgetting all the full Moon nights that the emergency room was not busier and all the extraordinarily busy nights that pop up nowhere near a full Moon. Similarly, if we are walking along a dark road with our headlamps on in a place where we expect to see an abundance of, say, lizards, and we spot a couple in the beam, then we might be tempted to think of that as support for our model, even if those were the only two lizards within a twenty-mile radius, a vast area our eyes had been blinded to by our light.

At the start of our stellar observing project, we would have claimed we were building this data set to look for apparent stellar brightening events that arise from gravitational microlensing, although we were well aware that many different things might show up, given that we were observing broadly, without headlamp focus. One way to envision Einsteinian general relativity as a model for gravity is to recognize space as a deformable substance that can be curved by massive objects. When light from a background star encounters the curved space, it changes direction. If the object bending space is sufficiently small, light that would have missed Earth can pass around all sides of the object and get deflected so that it hits us. That is, we see light that we wouldn't have seen without the small, dark microlensing object. The background star gets brighter, briefly. The brightening is short-lived because everything is moving relative to everything else, and our alignment with the dark object and the background star must be nearly perfect for the brightening to occur. Presumably there is a lesson in there for us. Keep moving and enjoy the brief light from chance alignments when they happen. These astronomical alignments should be rare, so rare that we wouldn't expect to see them in our data, but that's what would make it particularly interesting if we saw a few. Plus, to increase our chances to see them, we need to take very short images that don't use standard astronomical filters, causing the quality of the images to degrade. Oh yeah, we have one more strike against us. We wanted to be sensitive to objects in the outer solar system. Not objects that are known, mind you, or even theorized, but objects that might or might not be lying outside the headlamp beam. To make this work, we need to look in the plane of the solar system (maximizing our chances of encountering a solar system object) where it crosses the plane of the Milky Way (giving us a sufficient number of background stars for potential brightening). That crossing of planes only occurs low on our southern horizon, further degrading the images. And all sorts of random things can happen to make a star appear oh-so-briefly brighter. If people were being polite, really polite, they would have characterized the project as "quite ambitious." But we knew that with a data set so rich, we would see many other somewhat less exotic things, and the primary point was to get generation after generation of students awash in a data set that allows them to be doing meaningful exploration while learning astrophysical theory, computer programming, data analysis techniques, and statistics. If you think you have heard too much about Poisson counting statistics and histograms, just talk with one of them about how I go on and on. At least they only must endure the harangue for a few years. I'd call them long-suffering, but it only seems long to them.

Most, not all, of the projects these students have explored can be fit roughly into three main classes. We have already discussed long-period pulsating stars that we find. Apparent flare events in the stars we study also arise. Now these could be the microlensing events that first motivated us, but it is far more likely that they have to do with something happening on the stars themselves. This work has been challenging because it is largely about eliminating events that lack astronomical causes, like noise in the camera, as we look for an astronomical needle in a haystack of noise. The next class of projects involves objects known as eclipsing binary star systems. These look like a single star to our telescopes but are really two stars orbiting one another. If the orbit is aligned just so, then one star will periodically pass in front of the other, blocking some of the light from the star behind, causing us to see the apparent single star get dimmer. We have discovered several of these systems. The geometry is such that we are much more likely to find them if they are orbiting right on top of one another. Thus, we see stars interacting and we try to deduce the nature of that interaction from any changes to the timing of the eclipses. It's possible to think of this tiny patch of sky as a special place I hunt, an astronomical half section. I return to it as an old friend each spring to see what is the same and what has changed, just as I return to New Grandpa Place, Arroyo Place, and Old Homestead Place to do a similar analysis each fall.

The first of two turkeys I managed this year came from New Grandpa Place after I'd bagged a duck earlier in the morning. Likely related to my "fish thoughtfully and purposefully but appreciate whatever bites" approach to all aspects of life, I am particularly pleased when I bag two birds of very different species in a single day, birds lacking any obvious habitat or life history connection—like turkeys and ducks. I had just dropped onto the remnants of an old roadbed, presumably the logging road used to create the always unproductive clear-cut that I had just worked, unproductively, of course. Simultaneous with my arrival at the road seeking an easier way down the hill, a flock of turkeys emerged from the ravine on the far side, about fifteen yards below me. They too presumably sought an easier way up or down the hill. It was instant pandemonium, something worthy of a double-time police scene from *The Benny Hill Show* with circus music playing. As is often the case for me in these situations, a brief moment of clarity emerged, when I saw a single bird crisply, seemingly frozen apart from the multitude bouncing here and there in a frenzied buzz. At the shot, the bird rolled and rolled and rolled to the bottom of the far ravine, creating one of the most precarious retrieves I've ever known. Never have I felt more like an elk hunter, trying to figure out how to pick my way out with that bird.

The second turkey came the day after Thanksgiving, when I was, believe it or not, turkey hunting. I set up high on a hill near known turkey-roosting trees above a trout stream, one we haven't yet encountered. A companion stream to the Troutpalooza stream, this one is also wildly popular, so that we may think of the wildlife management area as Troutpalooza Place II. Long past when I was certain the birds would have departed the roost, I started back down the hill. Halfway down the farmer's road, sounds of turkeys flying down from roost emanated from the woods to my left. I slipped into the forest and got a bird. What made this another sign of plenty was that it was the sixth property I had taken a bird from this year, matching my record for the most property diversity in a season. Diversity of all sorts—species, properties, experiences—is an important measure, probably the most important measure, of a successful season for me.

This interest in diverse experiences is what makes me, briefly, like a microlensing brightening event, think following the lead of Jim Fergus would be great. Kristin and I have read and reread *A Hunter's Road*, Fergus's 1992 tale of hunting all manner of birds in a breathtaking variety of settings all across the United States, always with his lab, Sweetzer. It is a marvelous dream, and maybe someday we can bite off a little piece of it, but if the patchwork of experiences and activities that have been built into the pillars that support my existence have anything to say about me, it is that I am a homebody, preferring to visit the same patch of sky and the same half dozen local properties each year, watching each evolve, my eyebrows arching slightly as some new realization emerges regarding a friend that seemed as if it could hold no further secrets. While hunting prairie birds or mountain grouse in the most spectacular country this land has to offer, part of me would be wondering what the trees at New Grandpa Place looked like this week and whether the ducks were gone yet.

My woodcock for the year came on October 30, once again at New Grandpa Place. I started the morning set up to hunt ducks as they flew off, pretty normal. A group of seven came by just after first light, and I missed with both barrels—as I say, pretty normal. I had the gun broken open, shells in hand, when the next pair appeared. With no time to mess things up by thinking, I loaded, swung, and fired, dropping the bird neatly. Its momentum carried it past me into the heavy marsh grass so that it took fifteen minutes of searching to turn up that bird, despite my having marked it down very well.

Just before the ducks flew that morning, I'd heard the twitter of wings settle into the willows east of the pool. If not for the prior year's experience seeing woodcock drop in, I might have dismissed the twittering wings as something else or failed to notice them at all. Wood duck in game pouch, I went to the far end of the copse to start back through this interesting cover, working in the direction of the truck. These willows are tall, at a good ten feet. A heavy undergrowth makes passage difficult, and pools of water appear throughout, the largest being of enough area to hold ducks hoping to pass the day in hiding.

Three quarters of the way back, fresh whitewash and bore holes signaled that a woodcock had been there recently, leading to escalating tension with each step. Just as it seemed the tension might dangle there without resolution, two woodcock came up together, one flying straight away, headed for the next willow clump, the other bending out left toward open water. I swung on the second bird, killing it as it cleared the trees. This one I admired for a particularly long time, smoothing its feathers and studying its wings, bill, and feet before sliding it into the game pouch with the duck.

One week later, a trip up the hill to visit the Wily Woodcock lair was in order. Already the cut was showing signs of becoming too sparse. The birds would not be in the area much longer, although the bramble across the farmer's road remained decent cover. I was unsure whether I wanted to shoot a second bird in the same year from the same property, albeit a very different place on the property, as doing so would break one of my admittedly flexible rules. This dilemma led to me pondering abundance and scarcity and the richness of this place as I huffed and puffed my way up the hill. Of course, I needn't have worried about taking a second woodcock. After the clear-cut produced nothing, I eased out onto the arrowhead pointing across the valley. It was splashed with fresh whitewash. I was hunkered down, admiring this woodcock excrement, when the bird erupted more or less from right under my rear end. It was gone before I could stand, never mind turn and swing the gun. Wily Woodcock, 4; this hunter, 0.

YEAR 18

Larger Discontinuities

Kristin and I both had full-time administrative jobs at this time, giving a different rhythm to the year than the one that characterizes full-time teaching appointments. I taught a fair amount on top of my administrative load but was not teaching during the spring of this year. This oddity of schedule meant we had the opportunity to get away north for the weekend between the end of classes and commencement, a rare once-in-a-working-lifetime luxury. We departed after a Board of Regents meeting at the end of the day on Friday, straggling into a motel lobby near our favorite Minnesota river as the West Coast baseball game we were listening to reached the seventh-inning stretch. God bless satellite radio. The clerk was waiting anxiously at the door, explaining that there was a baby bird on the sidewalk, and she was trying to keep a lurking cat from eating it. She closed with, "I think it's a baby hawk." I did my best to help out by picking up the bird—maybe a house finch, but who knows when they are that small and fuzzy—and placing it gently in a tall bush at the far end of the sidewalk. Any cat that had been making a living on its own for any time at all surely saw me put the bird there and just as surely knew how to climb a bush. As I said, I did my best to help out.

The next morning, we fished the river for several hours before driving to close the day at our favorite northern Wisconsin tubing lake, where we fished until dark, every second of this trip precious like stolen time. As the sky darkened, two woodcock began a sky-dance competition nearly right on top of us. At least two more could be heard peenting nearby. This really did feel like a contest, in a way that a lone Iowa bird never did. Even closer than the woodcock was a whip-or-will, seemingly on a limb no more than a few feet above our heads. I've previously described the downward flutter of the displaying woodcock as a liquidy gurgle, which is how it sounds to me except when compared to a softly calling whip-or-will right above my head. Now, that's a liquidy gurgle. The place called us to stay until the show was over and the credits were rolling, but we were tired, with long months of an academic year behind us, long hours of fishing and travel on the day, and a long week ahead.

Later that summer, having deemed the firing of my gun too unreliable, somewhere along the line, we stopped at a major retailer (different from the one of the earlier gun purchase) and got a new 12-gauge over/under shotgun. This one didn't come with instructions for what to do if it didn't fire. It has been treating me well ever since, an even more functional work of art.

What a gift it is to be able to measure out the flow of life by year-to-year changes in encounters with wild birds—and maybe even more, to make a living talking to people about the nature of the universe. So many people never had the chance to get that far, and life can change in an instant because of catastrophic illness, destructive weather, accidents, or human-induced violence. Loss is everywhere. That must be the context for the challenge I confronted when I had reached the relatively mature age of fifty-two and had already experienced so much that life has to offer. Taking care of routine business before the academic year got firing, I visited the doctor in August. To be honest, my check-ups were occasional. I'd always been healthy and busy, and the seed for this one, my first in a few years, was likely planted on our June trip back to Wisconsin. Driving late at night, we were listening to an eighties music station when the famous radio personality reminded the world that we lost Dan Fogelberg to prostate cancer way too young and I thought, "It's probably time to see about my prostate." God bless satellite radio.

At the early morning doctor visit, I mentioned to my new physician (one other had retired and one left town, not my fault, I swear) that my PSA hadn't been checked in a few years, and it had always been on the high side, about 4, but stable. Once in the middle of a digital prostate exam, the physician had noted, "You certainly have a generous prostate." My new physician and I discussed my lack of symptoms, and she deduced that it was very unlikely that I had any serious problem, but we added a PSA test to the other blood work I was getting on the way out. Kristin and I then drove off to fish, taking care of still more important routine business before the academic year got firing.

When we got home, we saw the pharmacy had left a message saying my prescription was ready. My prescription was ready? This was odd. I had also missed a call from the clinic. I logged into the portal to discover that my PSA was now sixty-nine. Prostate cancer is a disease well-suited for reminding us that nearly all things are best thought of as situated somewhere along a spectrum. This cancer is common, typically indolent to the point that there has been serious discussion about whether, most of the time it appears, it should even be called cancer. That word carries a weight that leads to more angst and treatment than needed, a course of action that provides a nearly textbook example of the adage, "The cure is worse than the disease." For some time, experts have been pushing active surveillance (AS) as a first-line approach to most prostate cancers. In an AS approach, one waits to see what develops before committing to a treatment protocol that does lasting damage. Usually nothing develops, or it takes a long time to develop. But the word "cancer" is like a dagger to the American imagination. Men don't want to sit around knowing that thing, that word, is idling there inside them. They want it out, destroyed, wiped from the face of the earth. For a time, the recommendation was even to stop doing routine PSA screenings for anyone, an action designed to save American men from themselves. If they never knew that their PSA had crept up, say from four to seven, they could avoid being in the position to make a questionable medical decision. Routine PSA screening is still actively discouraged for men younger than 55, my demographic at the time of diagnosis. In "We've Never Really Understood the Prostate," a MedPage Today review of Ericka Johnson's 2021 book, *Cultural Biography of the Prostate*, Howard Wolinsky noted that at that time, "55% of US candidates with low-risk prostate cancer go on AS versus about 94% in Sweden."

I am a proponent of AS whenever feasible, but key to Wolinsky's report is the phrase "candidates with low-risk prostate cancer," reminding us that prostate cancer is not monolithic, and even though most cases are indolent, some are not. Our shared humanity envelops much commonality as well as breathtaking diversity. Always, those who display a characteristic that is somehow different from that of the majority are every bit as important as those who display the more common characteristic, and it can be no different with prostate cancer, perhaps one of the reasons there was significant pushback against the recommendation to cease routine PSA screening. A PSA of sixty-nine screams "not a candidate with low-risk prostate cancer," my prostate cancer having already invaded the lymph nodes and migrated to my hip bone. Therein lies another reason for maintaining PSA checks. Not "low-risk" means that the outcome could be very serious. It's another case of "better safe than dead," as the state vet had implied about rabies after my bat encounter.

My local clinic is part of the Mayo Clinic Health System, and we were able to get going quickly at the flagship clinic in Rochester, Minnesota, leading to a diagnosis of stage 4 prostate cancer. It took about a month to get to this diagnosis. In this case, stage 4 meant the cancer was metastatic because it had moved from the local prostate area. At that time, my recollection is the American Cancer Society listed thirty-nine months as the median survival time with this diagnosis, the median of any distribution meaning 50 percent of values are greater than the median value and 50 percent are below it. My urologist suggested that an aggressive multimodal treatment approach would make the median survival time more like five years. There is no single best way to describe a distribution. Means are skewed by outlier events, while medians don't tell you what the tails look like, whether getting past five years means likely getting past ten or not. In response, we have developed countless other measures to better communicate the nature of a distribution of values, but these measures are harder to interpret and harder to come by; to be determined meaningfully, larger samples are required. As a result, we often find only means and medians reported. Knowing only an estimate of median survival time meant that I had some guidance regarding the probabilities of a couple different outcomes but not much beyond that.

It is an accident of biochemical good fortune that I have never been a fretter, one to worry about what tomorrow will bring, pretty far out on the tail of that curve, which might be represented by something like Poisson counting statistics. Of course, developing aggressive prostate cancer in my early fifties is an accident of biochemical misfortune, pretty far out on the other side of that curve. I didn't stew about the diagnosis, although just how much I had built my life around long-term projects snapped into sharp focus for the first time. It's an outstanding way to build a life, the most appropriate way for me, likely resulting from another biochemical accident. Some people flit from one thing to the next, siphoning energy from change and motion. Others of us get that energy from a slowly opening flower. I spent twenty-two years in southern Indiana and ten in California, lured by the draw of astrophysics in a place with a long history of discovery. Where else would I have had the opportunity to be a teaching assistant for a junior-level thermodynamics class that met in the very room where Ernest O. Lawrence built the world's first cyclotron? With twenty-five years and counting in my current home, it is safe to surmise that I am not one constantly in need of knowing what lies over that next horizon. In addition to the long-term star-observing project and getting to know woodcock at a one-bird-per-year rate, Kristin and I are attempting to catch a fish from each of Iowa's ninety-nine counties, adding a few per year. With thirty-five of ninety-nine completed, this is a long-term project indeed. Even my gardening involves watching the establishment of berry bushes and perennial flowers over the long haul. My very first long-term project was "the hole." When I was about ten, two friends and I began constructing a lavish hole for no other reason than to watch a hole develop. We worked on the project for a few years, even landscaping with trees and shrubs around our excavation. We can see my penchant for long-term projects in the graphs I make, watching the histograms of dates a particular species of bird was taken fill in point-by-point, year-after-year, the graph condensing information from the story of learning about a place and a bird.

The thing about many long-term projects is that their elusive resolution often lies barely over the next horizon. In many cases, that's the point. We could insert some cliché regarding life or different aspects of life being about the journey rather than the destination. Each summer, my students and I will see some potential subtle shift in a star or population of stars, and I'll say, "Wow, we might really see what's going on here with just a few more years of data." But in a few years, that denouement has drifted on down the road. Something like catching a fish in each Iowa county has a clearly defined endpoint, and we could have imagined barreling ahead, ticking off county after county in a race to get them in, but that would have been antithetical to the spirit of the operation. Plus, other things needed attention and energy.

The six weeks between that initial PSA check and the final diagnosis was a blur of activity. While we were getting CT scans, biopsies, and bone scans done locally that would all need to be repeated in Rochester, I was preparing for the busy academic year ahead. We took one day to make an ambitious trip for our Iowa county fishing project, adding three counties, venturing about as far west as we could in a day trip that included three meaningful fishing stops. The bulk of that day was spent rolling over gravel roads in pothole country, marshland opening out in all directions. I couldn't help but wonder how my life would have been different had I found a job there in western Iowa, so close to where I ended up, yet not close at all. Maybe I never would have seen a woodcock, becoming a duck specialist or chasing pheasants and Hungarian partridge over these wide-open spaces. Of course, I might have taken a research job and landed in an urban area, losing all connection with the natural world. Like most Americans, I might have grown to believe that it was OK, good even, to eat only food I had never seen living. The thing is, I am sure I would have been happy, designing a great—just very different—life.

Along one of the gravel roads on this fishing outing, a rail tried to cross in front of us, and we plowed into it at full speed, feeling the loss as we do when we shoot one, but none of the reward of having a bird for rumaki. Headed back east later in the day, while awaiting our meal at a restaurant, we saw two old-timers hunched over, investigating the grill of our truck. After they had cleared the area, I thought I'd better go see what that was all about. It was about the pulverized remains of the rail, deeply embedded in the grill. I did my best to extract what I could and wandered around the parking lot trying to figure out what to do with the bird to show it a modicum of respect.

A week later, we added one additional western Iowa county to our "fish from every Iowa county" project, failing to succeed in two other brief stops. I nearly failed in the third county, catching a drum from a town park, but only after borrowing Kristin's rod so I could throw her lure for a few casts before accepting the failure. We were headed west for a total solar eclipse, the first of two that would be visible from large swaths of the United States in a seven-year stretch. It shouldn't be a shock to learn that I have never harbored a burning desire to chase eclipses around the world, as many people do. The steady flow of annual meteor showers and the motion of the planets against the background stars were more my speed. This eclipse was too close to let slip by unattended, totality passing fairly nearby and occurring before, although barely before, the onset of the academic year. We had the option to head west or south in search of totality. We opted for west, figuring the weather to be more reliably clear. The night before the big event, we stayed in Rapid City, South Dakota, planning to check the weather in the morning and drive on accordingly.

In the predawn of eclipse day, the highway south of Rapid City was busy with a stream of eclipse chasers. Much of the traffic peeled off west, headed for Wyoming, so we stayed south and landed at Fort Robinson State Park on the western edge of Nebraska, a place dripping with history, not exactly uplifting history, but real history, adding weight to the day. We parked early, spending several hours wandering the grounds and studying the exhibits, before finding a large field with nobody else around for show time.

I am a convert. Nothing in my life could have prepared me for that two-and-a-half minutes with the Sun fully blocked, despite the extraordinary astronomical orientation of my life for decades. As has happened frequently in my life, I understood something, a feeling, on a different level after a sudden experience, despite understanding the thing pretty thoroughly on an intellectual level prior to the experience. Seeing a woodcock sky dance for the first time is a great example. A life of rewarding slow-burn experiences that can be savored gently, punctuated with single dramatic events like this, is maybe not so bad. Kristin and I stood alone in our large field as the sky darkened and birds began flying to find somewhere to roost, like dusk but so unlike dusk, without any horizon glow, and the gloom gathering too rapidly, causing me to want to fly to roost as well. As I write, the next great eclipse is approaching rapidly, totality passing directly over my southern Indiana hometown, with a duration longer than what we had at Fort Robinson. The weather will be less reliable, and we will be right in the middle of a semester. Maybe it's worth figuring out how to make it happen.

In September, I made a trip to hunt rails and snipe in the marsh. The hunting season was threatened, to say the least, and I wanted to slip in one good day in the field. The rails were bunched up around a single water hole, more rails in a smaller space than I had ever encountered previously. Birds were flying everywhere, at least everywhere around that single water hole. The new gun performed admirably, and I bagged more in a day than ever before—or had ever wanted to before. Whatever else would happen that autumn, we would have our Thanksgiving rumaki.

It turned out that the season ahead was but marginally affected. The treatment plan included starting with androgen deprivation (hormone) therapy. That meant regular Lupron injections after an initial injection of Firmagon to hammer down the testosterone immediately. In terms of injection reaction, the Lupron was nothing like the Firmagon, which burned a fire through my abdomen and left hard cystlike structures that would occasionally erupt in fire many months later. I then would add a pill called Zytiga (abiraterone acetate) if we could get insurance to approve it. Zytiga suppresses testosterone in a different way, including working on the adrenal system, which required the addition of prednisone to the medicinal mix to counteract some of what we were losing. At that time, this approach was standard of care in Europe for disease like mine but was only approved in the US for relapsing disease. I think that has all changed now. My disease trajectory intersected the research trajectory at a specific moment before each trajectory continued onward. A different intersection would have led to a different treatment plan had I been diagnosed a year earlier or a year later. If we couldn't afford the Zytiga (about $10,000 a month), the alternative would be Docetaxel, a more commonly used chemotherapy drug. I'm not sure how it all worked, but I ended up on the Zytiga, in a patient assistance program, so that we paid almost nothing once we had reached our out-of-pocket limit. Yeah, the whole system seems pretty messed up. I suspect, however, that being on the Zytiga versus the Docetaxel helped save the hunting season. The goal was to suppress the PSA to a level below what could be detected by the standard test and hold it there for a few months. If the goal was met, surgery would remove the prostate, followed up with radiation therapy.

Saying that Zytiga saved the hunting season is not to say it was an absolute breeze. My blood pressure hovered around 150/110, with plenty of headaches that bordered on debilitating at times. I was a bit fuzzy and somewhat off. The next year, Kristin would say, "Oh that process is now done this new way. Don't you remember? We decided it in committee last year. It was your idea." I'd respond, "Uhhhhh." On the penultimate day of the turkey season, I headed to a large property that we have yet to encounter, a reminder that although Iowa has one of the country's lowest percentages of publicly owned land, I live in a blessed part of the state. In a shallow valley, I got turned around, not lost exactly, but not quite certain which was the best way to go or the precise direction of the parking lot. In our confined properties, with good landmarks, where I have been often, this just doesn't happen. As I was pondering my best path out, a turkey on the slope sauntered by me, disappearing behind a shield of brush before I reacted. In years past, it is a shot I would have made. Still, these effects are minor compared to what could have been.

I even managed two woodcock in October. The story of the first one should seem familiar (I won't say tedious, leaving that for the reader to say or politely refrain) by now. The day opened with duck hunting at New Grandpa Place. I missed my first two shots at groups coming off the pond. Sure, we'll blame the treatments. A bird fell with my third shot. It was jumping through the grass when I got to it, and twice I lunged and missed, perhaps a legitimate side effect of my physical and mental state. Thinking I heard a rustle a few feet away, I went to investigate, finding nothing. When I returned to the spot where I first encountered the downed bird, there it lay, expired. Maybe I was more addled than I realized. From there, I went through the willow copse where I got the previous year's woodcock. It sported ample whitewash, but I couldn't raise a bird. When I entered a different group of trees, far from the pool, a woodcock twittered up almost immediately. It was yet another time when I failed to see the bird fall to the shot, but the silence indicated it was down.

Two weeks later, the pheasant season opened, and I looked for birds on top of the hill at New Grandpa Place, stopping by Wily Woodcock land on the way up. On the outside edge, where the maturing aspen met the prairie grass, and where I first encountered woodcock up here, I heard a woodcock sort of half fly, as if it started to flush and thought better of it, the result being a sort of stutter skip or jump. Two steps more, and the bird curled out. The butt of my gun caught in my armpit as I tried to mount it, and the woodcock settled unscathed on the far end of the cut. As I approached once more, it shot across the farm road into the big woods and across the chasm. I fired once, watching as the woodcock disappeared from sight unharmed. It was the last woodcock I would see at this spot. Final count: Wily Woodcock, 5; this hunter, 0.

One day after my final Wily Woodcock encounter, two days before Halloween, I was working Arroyo Place, moving through the dry bed. A woodcock flew out to my left, headed for the seam between the woods and the prairie grass, continuing its arc to follow that seam back toward the parking lot and the stocking road where we had seen the woodcock rotating in complete circles as it peented. I was slow reacting. You can pretty much take that as true for the entire year, probably for the entire time since that year. Despite my sluggishness, I caught up with this bird, a second woodcock in a year that threatened to hold none. In its own way, this had been another year of plenty. As the hunting seasons did their annual crescendo from September through October, then faded into November and December before flickering out in January, my PSA number did its own fade from 69.3 to 3.1 to 0.18, before flickering out to undetectable alongside the hunting seasons.

Together Afield

I live some two miles from campus, my walk to work beginning about 6:00 every morning. In late March this year, I was nearing campus, lost in thought about who knows what, when I absent-mindedly noted the presence of a nighthawk, except there wouldn't be a nighthawk anywhere near for a couple more months. A woodcock was peenting along the road on the edge of campus. I watched him fly once before disrupting his display so I could walk past on my way to get settled at my desk. Two days later, Kristin and I caught one displaying at Arroyo Place, as had become an annual tradition. This one stuttered in flight, never gaining full altitude, seeming an awkward teenager just learning the ropes. We dubbed him Mr. Putt Putt.

Four days after watching Mr. Putt Putt, we were at the Troutpalooza II stream, trying with all we had to catch a fish, figuring my streak of consecutive months with fish or game taken would end at 240 if I didn't land something that day. All had gone well through the spring. With my PSA remaining undetectable, we were scheduled to drive to Rochester the following day for tests ahead of surgery. It was the beginning of what was to be a remarkably inclement April, bringing eight inches of snow over the two-and-a-half days we were in Rochester and another twelve inches a week later, along with temperatures anchored double digits below normal. This day at the stream was one we might not have fished and certainly would have given up sooner had we not felt the pressure of the streak. The icy wind roared as we tried to cast, unable to feel the line with fingers that were heavy, senseless blocks. Having tried almost everything in my box, everywhere we ever

caught fish on this stream, my thoughts were, "Ah, 240 months isn't a bad run." Driven by desperation, I put on a small crankbait to drag through the deepest part of the deepest hole around this area. Bam! Bam! Just like that, I had not one but two April fish. Kristin already had hers. The streak lived on.

Surgery was a success. "There was plenty of cancer left to get," the urologist told us afterward, in case we were somehow worried that surgery had been unnecessary given the PSA suppression that androgen deprivation therapy had provided. Having read many more metastatic prostate cancer research papers in the previous six months than I had astrophysics research papers, we harbored no such illusion regarding the lack of benefit of surgery. Because I wasn't a medical scientist, there were things I missed in the papers, but being a scientist and adequate with statistics, I got enough from them to be 100 percent on board with our treatment plan. Presumably my recovery was aided by my being twenty years younger than was typical for those who have the surgery, and I was back at work part time in about a week, ramping it up from there. Lifting and activity restrictions were in place well into May. Had I not caught those fish on April 1, it's unclear that I would have had it in me to get one before the calendar turned to May. We might have tried gentle "drive-up" fishing, but setting the hook with authority is so wired into my being, the chance that things could have gone very wrong was significant.

Before this surgery, I hadn't been hospitalized for nearly thirty years. My tonsillectomy had come a couple years after I spent a night in the hospital pretty sick from a kidney stone working its way through the system. In between these two years, I got a taste of my first real astrophysics research experience, when I spent my time cleaning and calibrating parts for a detector designed to fly on a high-altitude balloon hunting for antimatter heavy nuclei in the cosmic rays, nearly certain not to exist. But if they did exist, they would provide strong support for the existence of antimatter stars and thus a matter-antimatter balance in the universe writ large, instead of the matter dominance over antimatter we see in the local universe. Essentially, we only see relatively lightweight antimatter particles, and those particles are produced in high energy interactions in galaxies made fully of the stuff we think of as normal matter, that is, not antimatter. Nuclei of heavy elements like iron can only fly free through the universe after being produced in a supernova explosion, the cataclysmic end of a star. Nuclei of heavy elements made of antimatter would necessarily imply the existence of stars made of antimatter, or at the very least, a modification of our understanding of how heavy nuclei could be made.

The task I spent the most time on in that job was cleaning machine oil off a thousand delicate thin-walled metal tubes that would be used in a giant proportional counter array to track cosmic rays. I spent long days and long nights gently removing oil from each three- or six-foot tube, cataloging any small dents and carefully packaging the tubes for storage. It was mind-numbing work (perhaps less so after I started wearing a protective mask when dipping the tubes into an alcohol bath in a large vat I had constructed) and tedious by any standard, but it had to be done, and I was the one doing it. I was working on parts that would make measurements of cosmic ray particles. I was living the dream. In future summers, before heading to graduate school, I shifted to experimental nuclear physics and an entirely different type of experience in the lab.

The nuclear physics research group got access to the cyclotron's particle beam for a few short days of experimenting before relinquishing the beam to other researchers. The buildup to be ready for the beam and to make the most of the experiment was intense, capped by my role of lying in the scattering chamber feeding in liquid nitrogen supply lines, assuring that they did not touch the precisely aligned detector array as the two-ton lid of the chamber dropped slowly into place before I slithered out through a tiny hatch, having earned this task by being the smallest group member. The exhilaration of the time pressure in a particle beam physics experiment like that is something no other work experience has held. It was a time of boundless energy and limitless possibility, when it seemed as if it might genuinely be possible to connect all the dots, to understand everything, recognize the beauty of what it is all about.

I'd had one more overnight in the hospital four years after the tonsillectomy, during my third year of graduate school. It was, of all things, an intramural basketball injury that sent me to the hospital this time around. Another player and I were chasing the ball on its way out of bounds. In what I like to think of as a heroic feat of athleticism, I saved the ball to my teammates as the opposing player and I crashed to the floor in a heap. Standing to get back in the play, the first thing I noticed was my inability to close the fingers of my left hand. A quick examination of the situation made it obvious that the arm was swinging chaotically from a pivot point between the elbow and the shoulder. With play stopped, a teammate was asking to come out of the game for a rest. Because we only had six players, I was trying to say, "No. No. I need the sub," but no sound was coming out. Headed into mild shock, I sat down on the free throw line. Rec staff buzzed into action, providing a hard rolled-up mat as a pillow while dialing 911 and thrusting a waiver into my hand for signature proclaiming that they were in no way at fault and that I would not sue them. Even in shock I was thinking, "Sure, having someone sign a waiver *after* they are already injured and in shock is going to work."

The gymnasium had five parallel basketball courts with five games running simultaneously. Unfortunately, we were on the court all the way in, farthest from the door. When the paramedics—Karen, Kurt, and Kevin, I kid you not—arrived, they had to stop every single game to roll their gurney across to me. They started an IV drip to administer Lactated Ringer's or whatever isotonic crystalloid solution they used for shock in those days, all the while explaining calmly that they needed to call the emergency room doctor for permission to administer morphine before splinting the arm, and they really, really wanted to give me morphine. They made the call and received no for an answer. Knowing their stuff, Karen, Kurt, and Kevin told me that since they really, really wanted to administer morphine, we would wait five minutes and try the emergency doctor again. Once more, the word was no. Karen, Kurt, and Kevin explained they could only make one more attempt before we had to get moving. If the answer was still no, they would stuff a towel in my mouth for me to bite down on as hard as I could while they splinted the arm in record time. On the third call, we got permission for morphine. As I lay there, I could see the drops leaking into the IV line—one, two, three, and that was it, no more focusing my eyes, the ceiling tiles now an indistinct blur. I had some vague notion that my arm hurt, but there was nothing in the world I could have cared less about, and it was clear why Karen, Kurt, and Kevin had so wanted to administer that drug, how much easier it made their work. As they began the splinting process, the three Ks shouted in unison, "Don't try to help!" I have no idea what I might have been trying to do by way of offering assistance. The delay in getting the process started pushed us just past 9:00 pm, the threshold for an "after hours hazard" fee to be added to the ambulance bill. It was $800, almost twice what I was paying per month for my tiny slice of a dilapidated, shared, rent-controlled apartment, all for a two-mile ride through quiet residential streets.

As we got to the ambulance, so good was I feeling that I asked Kurt if maybe the arm was just sprained, not broken. He laughed right in my face, responding, "I'm pretty sure it's broken." En route to the hospital, we hit a pothole, causing the gurney to detach from its locking mechanism on the ambulance side, launching a nauseating wave of pain over me, worse than any discomfort that had come so far. Already, the morphine had lost its power, and I was worse for having had it. I understood a bit of the doctor's reluctance, and where I think I'd had a pretty good intellectual grasp of the concept of addiction previously, I now had at least something of an understanding of it on a different plane. I wanted more morphine. Likewise, when the metastatic cancer diagnosis arrived, I'd had a decent intellectual grasp of my mortality as well as the idea of the cycle of life on the landscape. I'd even had direct experience with the latter, but my new experience led to a different plane of understanding, knowing that the majority of people sitting in my seat wouldn't live more than another five years.

When the splint came off my broken arm, it was clear why Kurt had laughed, given the visually apparent spiral fracture of my distal left humerus. My muscles had clenched so that the top of the lower piece of the big arm bone had been pulled up even with or slightly above the shoulder, creating the visual effect of the kind of forked stick used for comic book sling shots. The doctor massaged the lower piece of bone back into place, and I spent a day hospitalized with the lower arm weighted to hold it in place before they sent me home. Afterward, I was treated by an orthopedic surgeon attached to the university, pictures of the football team adorning his office. He told me that everyone else in the practice would do surgery and insert a rod, but he'd prefer to let it heal naturally; if it worked, the bones would bond back together in a way that the upper arm would be straight. Given the knot that remains where the bones knitted, maybe this could have gone either way. I spent six weeks with my arm in a shoulder to hand cast tied to my waist, smelling like I had just come out of a basketball game. Afterward, I took my shriveled wreck of an arm to physical therapy, where the therapist did some baseline range of motion tests, having me raise my weak arm to touch my shoulder with my hand, slowly easing my hand down the back of my shoulder to see how far I could reach. "That's terrible," he said, pulling no punches. After a bit, he stopped and said, "Wait a minute. Let's try that range of motion test with your other arm." The results were nearly identical.

As well as prostate surgery turned out, the day didn't start perfectly. To go ahead with surgery an MRI needed to demonstrate tumor shrinkage in both the prostate and the hip bone. Shortly after that demonstration a surgery slot opened unexpectedly. Great! I had my April fish. Work was covered. I'd be back to full functioning power in time for commencement and the best lake fishing of the year. The morning of the surgery, Kristin had a fine motel breakfast, and we wandered the few blocks to the hospital through the snowstorm. There, we checked in at the lobby and settled into a large, airy waiting area for a modest wait before we were called into an office for the process to get underway, or so we thought. It turned out that the procedure had yet to be approved by insurance and we risked being liable for the full bill if we went ahead. Medically, the delay of a month or so would mean little. The Lupron and Zytiga were still doing their thing, and if they stopped doing their thing in the next month or two, well, then, the surgery wasn't going to do us much good anyway. But we were prepped and ready to roll.

We returned to the big, open waiting area, and Kristin got on the phone with our HR director, who got on the phone with her connection at the insurance provider. We waited and kept getting bumped down the surgery list, knowing that once we slipped past a certain point, it would be too late, and we'd need to reschedule. I don't know how close a call it was, but we made it, presumably with minimal time to spare. Prep room, prep room 2, prep room 3, and I was in the operating room. Next thing I knew, I was in recovery, with no indication that they didn't get all the local cancer. The cancer that had already traveled to the hip bone would need to await radiation therapy. Only one of twenty-one lymph nodes extracted and biopsied had cancer, not as good as none, but a heck of a lot better than a few or several.

I spent almost exactly the same amount of time in the hospital with a broken arm on which we decided to forego surgery as I did after having a chunk of my urethra removed in an old-fashioned open (not laparoscopic or robotic) prostatectomy. My recovery was rapid. I had taken my first walk down the hall before they settled me into bed after arriving from post-op. Still, I had expected to spend more than a single night in the hospital. If these decisions are a linear combination (e.g., $0.6 \times A + 0.4 \times B$) of medical decision and insurance company decision, it's hard to know what the weighting factors are. On the one hand, I'm a big proponent of spending the bare minimum time required in the hospital. I figure if things are going to go wrong in terms of infection, the hospital and the woodcock–wood duck marsh are two likely sources; it's just the one from the hospital might be a lot harder to kick. On the other hand, I was pretty feeble twenty-four hours after an open prostatectomy, when they informed us that I was being dismissed while my Jackson-Pratt drain was running stronger than the field tile that has destroyed so much seasonal wetland around these parts. After the notice of dismissal came in, we sat around waiting for the dismissal to be finalized as one hour became two, and two became several. The nurse apologized profusely for getting pulled away and causing the multihour delay, but I suspect that she—like Karen, Kurt, and Kevin—knew her stuff and was intentionally delaying to give me more time before the seventy-five-minute ride home. Once home, the first few days of recovery were a little touchy, but I was back at work, very part-time light duty, when most websites suggested that I might still be in the hospital. Unfortunately, any chance of watching the woodcock mating display was over for this year.

The cat and the dog reacted in different ways as I convalesced. The dog, a miniature poodle, understood her job to be to comfort. Very good at her job, she wanted to be on my lap desperately, never understanding why she wasn't allowed. The cat, a vagrant who had shown up at the house one Halloween and graciously accepted the invitation to give up chipping sparrows as sustenance for the life of indoor luxury, was more worldly. She regarded me as having survived an epic battle for existence. Perhaps I had. Kristin and I have a favorite story from *Gray's Sporting Journal* called "The Two Bears" by Kurt Cox. It's a tale of a bear hunter interacting with two different bears, one of them a huge old bruin called Big Chocolate. We imagined the cat thinking something like, Oooh, good job. Big Chocolate did a number on you, but you must have fought well to make it through.

I typically start taking images of our patch of sky one week either side of the first of March. At that time, our field of interest rises shortly before sunrise, and I can get my data by heading to work an hour or two earlier than normal. Because you hang on my every word, no doubt you recall that the rotation period of Earth is approximately twenty-three hours and fifty-six minutes, while our day is four minutes longer at twenty-four hours. The stars are all so distant that our little bit of movement in orbit during one rotation has no discernible effect on where they appear to us. The patch of sky we study will return to the same spot in the sky after one rotation— twenty-three hours and fifty-six minutes later. That is, the stars rise four minutes earlier each night, so that the time for the start of data collection gets four minutes earlier each day, until we get to October, when there is insufficient darkness while our field is visible to the telescope to get meaningful data before our 1,650 stars disappear below the observatory wall.

With the impending surgery and my general lack of energy, waiting until postsurgery recovery in May or June to start the data season seemed the best option. We got a few nights in June, and it was glorious to be back at the observatory, but clouds hampered July and early August until it was obvious that we would not get sufficient data this year to do anything with it in terms of our ongoing research. I gave up and rested instead. It is the only year missing from our two decades of research, a missing year I wouldn't have dreamed possible just a few years earlier.

Five months spanned the gap from surgery to the first days of hunting, and I had largely recovered when I took to the fields, although I was functioning at a noticeably lower level than the year before, and a rougher season all around was the result. Surgery surely played a role, but I suspect the full year of androgen deprivation therapy was taking a larger toll, maybe something like $0.2 \times$ surgery $+ 0.8 \times$ ADT, if we are trying to make our best guess at a linear combination of effects again. My muscles had atrophied to an extent that I couldn't hold my shoulders square. They curled forward like a potato crisp to give me the appearance of a severely sunken chest, and my upper back ached while my legs spasmed vigorously with the slightest or no exertion. If it sounds horrific, then I have oversold things. By most measures, certainly compared to what might have been, life was good, despite hunting and nearly everything else being far from trivially easy.

In different circumstances, I might be looking back on this year as special for dove hunting. I was in the birds, getting looks at close range far more than in previous years. The primary problem was that I was missing at a spectacular rate. Finally, I held my position after pulling the trigger in an effort to dissect what was going on. After a particularly galling miss, I detected that my cheek wasn't down against the gunstock sufficiently. If the gun mount had been like this each time, any hits I'd had (and I'm not actually sure I'd had any at this point) were either luck or the result of an errant pellet like the one that dropped the second duck on opening day at Old Homestead Place years earlier. Not that this was a surprise, given that my neck was so stiff I couldn't turn it to do a proper head check when backing up the truck. Focusing hard on getting cheek to gun, I downed a couple of doves before they were completely scattered off the public land. My shooting remained improved as fall progressed, but one will never achieve great shooting outcomes when one is concentrating hard on gun mount and head position instead of the flying target.

Without question, the best part of the hunting year was Kristin's deciding she wanted to be part of the hunting experience. She has taken to it and is now not only my constant fishing companion but also my constant hunting companion. There's no doubt she had interest in the activity, although I can't help but wonder whether, this first year, she also wanted to keep an eye on me as I staggered around the woods. On one of our frequent trips to Rochester, we got her a 16-gauge that she could handle well but that was not ideal for her, never fitting quite right, with a stiff safety and feeling a little whippy. She has for the most recent season switched to a 20-gauge pump gun that had belonged to my dad, and it works well for her.

Kristin's first hunt occurred on fall break at Big River Place. We walked the clear-cut where I had shot a woodcock with my dad before it had been recut. By this time, it was again good woodcock cover, actually already a bit long in the tooth, suggesting that we should have checked in with it a year or two earlier, but there are more heavenly places to visit on Earth, Horatio, than time and energy to visit them, or something like that. For Iowa, it is a sizable clear-cut, clinging to a hillside sufficiently steep that it provides a fun picture, imagining what doing the cutting must have been like. The cut starts near the gravel road, extending two-thirds of the way up the hill. Halfway up into the cut, there is a path that served as a logging road and has been maintained as a snowmobile trail. For her very first time out as a hunter, Kristin decided to keep the gun unloaded while walking this trail as I busted the clear-cut below the trail on our journey out and above the trail as we returned. About half an hour into the hunt, a woodcock that I had walked right past flushed ten yards behind me and swung uphill as I was too entangled to spin the 180 degrees—well, really 240 degrees by the time I would have caught up to the bird— to make anything like a reasonable attempt. The bird flew across in front of Kristin, offering one of those rare slow-motion crossing views in the wide open. We decided she would load her gun for the rest of the hunt, but that was our lone bird of the day.

Kristin's transition to being a hunter was aided by late summer having tilted toward the very wet, and River Wetland Place was experiencing one of its on years. Ducks were flying, giving me ample opportunity to practice getting cheek to stock and for Kristin, who had zero hunting experience, to see birds on the wing. Like us, the place had changed since I first wet waded the muck to retrieve teal more than a decade earlier. Mostly, sandbar willows were behaving true to form, and that little pool where I got those teal and enjoyed sitting over decoys was now almost choked out by colonizing willows, great for wood ducks, less so for teal and mallard, but the teal and mallard still used the space some. Mostly the changes meant that there was very little opportunity to decoy, leading us to pass shooting almost exclusively. The wing shooting challenge of pass shooting is distinct from that of a dogless hunter flushing birds in the woods, although quick identification of the situation and a fluid reaction are key to each. The advantage I have in the flushing situation is that I have been doing it for forty-five years. I've seen a lot of birds take off without warning over all those

decades, and although each flush is still a thrill, my body reacts well
without cognitive prompting. An advantage over Kristin I have in
pass shooting is that my hearing is better, or at least more attuned
to the sounds of the hunt. Without conscious recognition of what is
happening, I hear wings approaching and am calculating a trajectory
so that my feet are reacting and my shoulders already turning when
the duck emerges over the trees at full speed, there for a brief moment
before disappearing behind another screen of trees.

Kristin and I have talked about the advantages and challenges of
learning something completely new after age fifty, and I am not sure
I could do what she is doing, learning to recognize all the hunting
situations sufficiently quickly to make a shot while attempting to
master the mechanics of shotgunning and always, always thinking
safety first. When I was ten years younger than she was when she first
picked up a shotgun, I taught myself bass guitar. Well, I hesitate to say
I taught myself to actually play, but my wife abides my presence as I
plunk along, with her on concertina, and we have fun. One goal was
to exercise my brain-body connection in an entirely new way, much
as Kristin is doing now. It was excruciating at times, my brain having
to think so hard that my body couldn't react in any kind of fluid way
and my hands not as nimble as they were twenty years ago, however
feebly nimble they were then. That's the downside of tackling this kind
of challenge at an advanced age, the body failing to react as it did when
younger. The advantage of age is wisdom, or at least an enhanced ability
to learn from observation and study. When I was trying to learn how
to make a bass guitar work, I could read for understanding, compiling
a background through words, as I observed others playing, watching
for detail that could be translated into something meaningful for me
in a way I would not have been able to when I was, say, twelve. But
the twelve-year-old me had the physical ability to just keep hammering away at it. I suppose hidden in there is something of what people
mean when they say, "Youth is wasted on the young."

Another adage related to all this late-in-life learning goes, "You can't teach an old dog new tricks," to which people react, sometimes forcefully, that this is absurd, and of course you can continue to learn new things. Evident here is the tendency (need?) for people to think in hard binaries—or, if you will, not false but unnecessary dichotomies. People have heard of false dichotomies and likely have been warned off them, but they are ingrained in us. We teach them to children from a young age: "Slow and steady wins the race." As an instructor of kinematics, I am here to report that fast and steady beats slow and steady 100 percent of the time, steadiness and speed being a false dichotomy. Another false dichotomy that has seeped into our collective being is the idea that it is good to "work smarter not harder." My students have foisted that one on me regularly as they attempt to explain some clever new approach to data analysis. I patiently explain to them that the universe isn't likely to reveal its secrets unless they figure out how to work harder *and* smarter *and* harder.

If dichotomies are real—young and old, learning and not learning—they still often aren't that helpful. There is no hard dividing line between young or old or even learned and not learned or for that matter maybe not always true and false. It's typically not that we learned A and not B, but that we learned some aspects of A to a certain degree while we likely learned some aspects of B to a certain degree. If we learned fewer aspects of B and to a lesser degree, we can fall into the trap of saying we learned A and did not learn B, the hard binary of learned / not learned not being particularly helpful in our analysis. Don't even get me started on whether I care if Pluto is or isn't a planet. So whether you think an old dog can learn new tricks might depend less on the dog and tricks in question than on what you mean by "learn" and "old."

My woodcock for the year came three days after Halloween from Troutpalooza Place, the clear-cut atop the hill having neared a perfect age to hold woodcock but still too thick for easy traversing or shooting. We began the morning by leaning against large oaks, listening for turkeys awakening to greet the day. It was the morning of the now famous "squirrowl," an animal of myth we still speak of in hushed tones whenever we are near the area. As light started to build, I could make out the silhouette of an owl at the crook where a large limb intersected the main trunk of a tree, the head and ears protruding above the stout body of what appeared likely to be a screech owl. I was enjoying this rare moment when the animal suddenly moved, making it clear I had been observing a squirrel the entire time. Appearance, especially in low light, can be deceptive. I suspect I would have an easier time convincing some people of the squirrowl's existence than the snipe's existence.

At 8:00, after hearing no turkeys, we donned blaze orange and looped the grass for pheasants, raising none of those either. The pheasant hunt was planned to deposit us at the very top of the clear-cut so we could work it back toward the truck and call it a good day of the kind of mixed hunt northeast Iowa can provide. The large size and density of the cut caused us to work to near exhaustion. Eventually, Kristin moved out into the grass for easier walking as I plowed through the thick stuff. A bird, apparently reacting to my thrashing through, escaped the edge of the woods without my having any inkling it had flown. It's one of those times when you wonder if this sort of thing has been going on your entire life while alone on the hunt or in other aspects of life when something important and beautiful slipped away without any recognition it had been there in the first place. Kristin flushed the bird farther out into the grass, again without my having any clue this was going on. When I emerged, bloody and thrashed, she explained all this to me before we worked the grass meticulously, unable to raise the bird. For the final walk out, I was up against the brush row where my other gun had first failed on that pheasant years ago as Kristin stayed twenty yards down into the grass. Halfway through the field, a woodcock flushed from the brush row. As the cover was too thin for a woodcock, it's nearly certain that this was the bird that had been in the grass, it having scurried into the sparse woods as we tromped around the prairie. I made a clean shot and shared the moment of holding the bird and admiring the feathers, feet, eyes, and bill in the field with my wife for the first time. It was the first woodcock I'd shot with someone else present in many years.

The bird hunting season ended in December and January with my getting daily doses of radiation therapy. We gave it all we had, ensuring that the prostate bed, pelvic lymph nodes, and the spot on my hip bone all received as much radiation as deemed tolerable.

Recall that stars start their lives fusing hydrogen into helium in their cores, the innermost regions being the only place with sufficient temperature and pressure to propel the protons close enough to one another to allow the fusion to happen. After the hydrogen in the core has been entirely converted to helium and the fusion ceases, the inner layers of the star will contract. That contraction heats those interior layers, and fusion of hydrogen into helium in a thin layer around the core begins. For heavy stars, think ten or twelve times as big as the Sun, it is possible to keep fusion going, manufacturing the chemical elements of the periodic table all the way up to iron, building an iron core that is getting ever hotter as more iron falls inward, converting some gravitational potential energy into thermal energy. Among these are the pulsating variable stars we study in our data set. At some point, the star's core is sufficiently hot that the photons it is emitting break all those iron nuclei back into individual protons and neutrons, setting off a process that will yield a supernova that unleashes a shockwave ripping out through the star, destroying the star but also creating all the elements of the periodic table, elements well beyond the iron that once formed the stellar core. The shockwave continues into space, where it can trigger the collapse of a gas cloud, the collapse yielding new stars. These stars are enriched with all sorts of heavy elements, including the carbon that I take from a woodcock. Cycles within and on top of cycles. Before the supernova, the star spent millions of years building its iron core. The core was photo-disintegrated in less than a second.

It took me two pelvic radiation therapy sessions to undo decades of progress in controlling my irritable bowel syndrome that had reached a zenith after my tonsillectomy and that I had eventually learned to, if not control, then dance with nimbly, more or less without conscious thought. Now, three years out from those first two radiation therapy sessions, I begin to suspect that the earlier stasis shall never quite return.

I usually wore a tie to these radiation therapy sessions. Wearing a tie isn't all that uncommon for me, as I often don one for work, despite my being about the only one who does so, like being the only one who hunts snipe and woodcock around these parts. During radiation treatment, when I was naked from the waist down and being jostled about to get my alignment tattoos just right, the shirt and tie made me feel a bit more human. So there I would be, half naked and half overdressed, while the radiation therapist struggled to maneuver me into correct alignment so we would get exactly the number of high energy photons exactly where we wanted them to be. A smile would cross my face, reminded of Karen, Kurt, and Kevin, when midprocess she would shout, "Don't try to help!"

YEAR 20
Focus

I suspect that if we had the ability to really know the people around us and made the effort to reflect on that knowledge, we would be startled by all the seeming incongruity that would turn up, as with me looking for wood ducks and woodcock together. It's just too easy to find a label, like specialist or generalist, and move on, when the reality is more likely that any person or thing has aspects of each characteristic in some linear combination. My project of watching the same small patch of sky is a fine example. It's hard to imagine something with greater focus than watching the same tiny patch of sky with the same 1,650 stars year after year after year. Yet somehow we find novel projects for students to complete each year, some closely related to earlier projects, but some wildly new, with multiple projects always ongoing and several more idling nearby, so that I likely have a wider array of disparate projects than the vast majority of astronomers in the world. An upside of that variety is just how interesting and fresh each day can be. A downside is that I feel like an interloper, not quite expert in any one thing we are doing. So it has been with my outdoor experience. A hard focus on a handful of properties near home must seem dreadfully boring to some, but the variety of experiences that spin out of these properties can make each week feel like opening day anew.

If a less than ideal narrow focus is to creep into any single hunting season, stripping away the unfolding of that ongoing opening day feeling, then the culprit is likely duck hunting, because duck hunting often goes well, with plenty of interesting birds around. Plus, it has an "expires on" date, when the ducks blow out to the south, but because that date is hidden and varies year-to-year, my inclination tilts toward continued driving at the ducks, the recognition that it could all be over tomorrow serving as the engine propelling that drive. Maybe that's how we are with many things in life, pushing too much in one direction for fear of missing out, or maybe we don't push enough on the things we love, not quite recognizing that it could all be over tomorrow. As with most things, it's likely a little of both. Another aspect is at play here. Long ago, we attempted to fully give up eating farmed animals for holidays and other special meals. If the duck hunting is good and birds are going into the freezer, sticking with it helps assure that culinary goal can be met. Once, when I was in graduate school oh so long ago, I was drifting down the hallway lost in thought when a colleague I had barely recognized was there grabbed me by the shoulders and playfully shouted, "My God man, where is your existential angst?" I imagine that without my culinary motivation, I would be perfectly content to wander far and wide through the woods and fields, barely concerned with whether I raised a bird or not, soaking in the world around, all while sporting the same vaguely vacant smile that my face must have shown all those years ago in the hallway outside my office, a space where Oppenheimer first met with prominent scientists from across the country to discuss the potential for building an atomic bomb while armed guards stood at the door to the room that would become my office half a century later.

I am nudged farther in the duckly direction if it is wet enough for River Wetland Place to be in play. This was a second consecutive such year, and our resistance to its pull waned from what it had been the year before, at least in part because birds were plentiful, and as Kristin learned this new thing of hunting, plentiful birds is what it would take for us to keep moving forward. Consistency of flying birds would be far more valuable for progress toward this goal than a new experience every week. We may have also been inflicted with a sort of duck drunkenness, given that this is the only time that we have had water at River Wetland Place in two consecutive years. Indicative of my struggle for balance, 71.4 percent of my birds this year came from this property.

It was also a year of my seeking normal. After surgery the previous year, we had discontinued Zytiga after radiation therapy, and we had let the Lupron injection lapse after a total of nineteen months of androgen-deprivation therapy. By the time hunting seasons began appearing, I had been off treatment for four months, still several months shy of any testosterone rebound I would enjoy, and even further short of my muscle tone returning in any significant way, but the process was moving forward. For the first time in what felt like a much longer time than it actually was, I headed afield without the immediate influence of medication.

This fall, I was, in my addled assessment, better off than I had been a year earlier, but my strength was short of where it was a couple of years before, although it might have been short of that mark anyway given that I was aging. Who knows how much strength I would have at this age without cancer and treatment. What I do know is that it is possible to make a hunt at River Wetland Place as physically challenging as one likes by pushing vast areas of grass and willows, but it's also possible to walk the dike in, albeit a long distance, to do some pass shooting without an abundance of exertion, something that appeals to me more than it did eight or ten years ago. Perhaps, instead of two consecutive huntable years at the River Wetland Place being a sign of more Upper Midwest deluges in a time of warming, it was a sign of the universe being kind to me. Sure.

Our first day at River Wetland Place, just after the calendar turned to October, produced swarms of ducks flying hither and yon, starting during the first quarter hour past the onset of legal shooting time. A group of five came barreling in from the direction of the river, and I hit one, the duck careening in and contacting the earth with a heavy thump, the bird's momentum having carried it well past us, into thick marsh grass. With the final twenty feet of the duck's descent screened from us by a stand of willows, we didn't see it hit, never a good omen for bird recovery, and half an hour of kicking turned up nothing. Losing the first duck of the season is about as bad as it gets, far worse than not seeing ducks, and introduces all sorts of doubt regarding what we are doing. A week later, the temperature had turned sharply colder, and we were wearing gloves far too early in the season. Again, my shots were at ducks coming from the river side of the dike, not the most common occurrence there. After a couple of early misses, I got a beautiful drake woodie that nearly hit me as it fell. That bird was followed by a blue-winged teal, a special bird ever since the lack of willow-free water had made teal so much less common here. Another highlight came later in the season, when Kristin and I were hunting a far end of the property, a location new for us. It provided good shooting opportunities because it was a particularly wet year, and this far end was now a sea of flooded dryland grasses as well as the largest willow thicket on the property. After taking a bird at first light, we were posted up, each in a different clump of willows separated by about forty yards, when a duck came in high on my side and I made one of my better shots of the year, the bird dying in the air with wings spread instead of folded, so that it helicoptered gently to the marsh in the trees behind me. With so much varied activity, you see how it could be hard to leave to hunt other birds, say woodcock. The last duck of the year at River Wetland Place was also memorable, once again coming from the new end of the property. The birds were boiling out of the willows, headed for the river or beyond at first light as Kristin and I stood with our silhouettes hidden by the dike behind us. A group banked by us in tight, arcing right to left, and I knocked one down. It drilled in hard near Kristin, and I thought it had landed between us. She heard it hit just past her. In the low light, there was no obvious evidence of the bird in the long grass covering the face of the dike. Crawling on hands and knees, I found first one, then two more blood spots on the grass of the dike, not the first time I have blood trailed a duck like an arrowed deer. Those minute crimson drops led to a beautiful, camouflaged hen woodie buried deep in the grass.

The best hunting day of the year had unfolded two weeks prior to that final duck. We started the morning on our "old" end of the property, where I got a duck from one of the early flights of birds headed back in from the river direction. When things settled, we moved to the new end of the property, where Kristin posted at the dike while I made a wide loop designed to pinch most of the willows between us before I started a slow push back, aiming to drive some birds her way. Barely into my drive, a group flushed nearby, resulting in my second stunning drake wood duck of the day, after which the birds began busting out well ahead of me. My limit came with a hen from a group circling back into the willows directly overhead. After emerging from the woods and making the long slog through the flooded grass to the dike, I found Kristin with her first ever bird, our fourth wood duck of the day. I was elated that we had executed our plan to near perfection, pushing escaping ducks past her, but disappointed I had been in the thick of the trees, unable to witness her shot. We ate two of the ducks from this day for Thanksgiving and the other two for Christmas, so warm it was at Christmas that we grilled them over charcoal after a soak in a commercial marinade purchased in powder form. They were spectacular.

Wednesday of fall break, sandwiched squarely between Kristin's first bird and my last duck of the season, found us able to pull ourselves away from ducks for some woodcock hunting. We ended the day at Big River Place, where we pushed the clear-cut, Kristin following a woodcock she could see waddling along in front of her. It slipped away without ever flushing, nor did any others fly on our walk away from the truck. We got four flushes from at least two different birds, likely three, headed back toward the truck. I took one long shot when a bird got up in the treetops, making it visible, but did not connect. We had begun the day at Old Homestead Place where we worked a narrow strip of heavy cover bordered by a field on our left and the farmer's access road on our right. It was a strip barely wide enough for both of us to hunt. Near the end of the cover, a woodcock flew across a small entrance road to the field and dropped into heavy cover on the other side, just short of private land, offering no chance for a shot. Going in for the reflush, Kristin hunted to my left. The bird got up to my right and curled toward the main farmer's access road. I fumbled with the gun as if I had never done this kind of thing before but managed to get on the woodcock and drop it on the edge of the road, both flushes of this bird having been less than twenty yards from where I had shot my second woodcock the year I had my bag checked by the conservation officer. Suddenly, I recognized how much nostalgia was playing a part in my hunting. The bird from Troutpalooza Place the year before had brought a nostalgic feeling because it was a throwback property for me, but that feeling wasn't nearly as strong as the nostalgia I felt with this bird at this spot where I'd bagged my second woodcock eighteen years earlier and just a mile from where I'd bagged my first the year before that. Being uninterested in pursuing unnecessary hard dichotomies, I won't go down the road of trying to determine whether this wallowing in reminiscence is good or not so good overall. More than anything, these birds remind me of how long I have been at this and the malleability of time. I suspect most readers of sufficient age recognize the compression of time as we get older. When I was young in the 1970s, the 1950s seemed impossibly remote, with funny clothes, odd hair, and strange cars. My childlike ears couldn't even connect the music of that earlier era with the rock and roll I was being raised on. In those days, about as much time separated me from the 1950s as now separated the two woodcock from this one field entrance road. The world had changed in myriad ways between those birds, and yet it seemed so little time had passed and that so much was fundamentally the same, not just back to that other bird, but back to people who walked this land when the old homestead was built, back to when people walked this land before any Europeans ever dreamed the place existed, back before any people knew of this land or even before this land was this land. It was as if none of my life had existed outside the span between those birds, and yet the time between those birds was but a blink of an eye.

Always Novelty

Were I the type to pick up and move every half decade, getting acquainted with new people, new societies, new land, instead of staying rooted in place, I would surely know a lot more about a wider slice of our world than I do now. Even if I merely traveled more, my knowledge umbrella would have a wider span. What might be missed, however, is the subtle texture that rides atop the basic understanding as well as the recognition of slow evolution. I fear that if I hopped from place to place, I might be even more inclined to slip into the "as it is now it always has been and always will be" trap. Plus, there might actually be less genuine surprise. When you know next to nothing about a place or a thing or a person, you're unlikely to be terribly surprised because you have no idea what to expect, or at least you should be open to the possibility that what you expect might be well wide of the bullseye of reality. Even the smallest unexpected event in one of my astronomy data frames or at one of the properties we have been visiting repeatedly in this tale has the ability to delight me, meaning we have circled back to where we were near the beginning, the idea that it probably isn't wise to do the same thing over and over again, expecting exactly the same result. In the spirit of full disclosure, I should note that I have the ability to be surprised by things I have seen before and that do not change or that lack the appearance of change, like the way seeing the three stars of the Summer Triangle—Deneb, Vega, and Altair—in the evening sky in December always captivates me; they are, after all, the *Summer* Triangle. Then, when I see Vega rising in the east the next icy morning after watching it set in the west the evening before,

I am doubly delighted, even though I understand the geometry and mechanics of rotation and orbit that make these things work.

We should pause to note that the Summer Triangle is, in fact, changing. Seen projected on the sky, all stars are moving very slightly relative to one another—this is known as proper motion of the stars. We don't notice their moving because the rate of change is so slow. In about a hundred thousand years, the handle of the Big Dipper will have folded in the middle and the bowl will be more like a scoop. Our view of the sky also changes because of precession of Earth's rotational axis around its orbital axis. A spinning top will wobble, or precess, around the vertical as it slows. Because Earth has an equatorial bulge, like a top, the gravitational pull from the Sun and Moon on that bulge leads to precession, with Earth's rotational axis sweeping out one complete loop in about twenty-six thousand years. Our north star, Polaris, the end star in the Little Dipper's handle, is important not because it is particularly bright but due to its location nearly on our rotational axis, thus pointing the way to geographical north. Because our rotational axis is sweeping out a loop, it has not always pointed in the direction of Polaris and is moving away from it now. In thirteen thousand years, Polaris will be about forty-seven degrees away from the pole.

As much as Kristin and I are homebodies, diving deeply into our local properties, we traveled even less than usual this year—as in not at all. We opted to stay close to home because COVID-19 made travel a challenge, but we also needed to stay close to the dog who was getting up in years and suffering from congestive heart failure. Regular around-the-clock attention and adherence to routine appeared to be the primary things keeping her going—well, those and Lasix, Vetmedin, Carprovet, Enalapril, and Mirtazapine. Ahhh, here's a chance for us to think in terms of linear combinations again. Our staying near home could be modeled as A times pandemic + B times dog health, where A and B sum to 1, the estimated linear combination that we have played around with previously. We weren't likely to take many overnight trips because of the pandemic, but we were also limited in our ability to take day trips designed to add Iowa fishing counties to our growing total because the dog needed attention at least every six hours or so, all this adding up to our visiting local lakes far more often than usual throughout the year.

One result of this attention to local lakes was that largemouth bass was our most common species caught for the first time in years. More important was the intimate feel we gained for bass behavior on these lakes throughout the year, the lakes growing to mimic the woodcock woods and duck marshes of autumn, where weekly investigation allows us to keep in close contact with how bird behavior changes as seasons wear on. It was a gratifying surprise to experience that with bass at the lake, noting bass reaction to weed growth, subtle shifts in preference for reaction-strike lures versus finesse lures or topwater plugs versus bottom-bumping plastics. A couple of things need to be pointed out. First, this evolution of bass behavior throughout the year must be viewed as a shift in what we experienced on average, with any one day still offering a high probability of surprise. Our close attention to detail allowed us to map those unexpected responses to things like weather shifts. Also, this was one of those times when I knew very well on a broad intellectual level how bass behaved in different situations. After all, for a few years when I was in high school, I was a black bass snob the way some people are trout-on-flies snobs. For a bit, I wanted nothing to do with fishing for anything but bass, bass, bass. That changed long ago, and as with my hunting, diversity of experience is at or near the top of the list of what I seek when fishing. But in my formative years, when observation and reflection could leave the most indelible mark on my view of the world, bass behavior was being imprinted there deeply.

Certainly, nothing was novel or unexpected about where we were flushing woodcock during October, as a few flew from the willows down low at New Grandpa Place on three different days, spread over a couple weeks. As can often be the case, especially when the forest is still fully leafed out from floor to treetops, things just didn't work out for us to connect with our bird there. We flushed a single bird from the now mature clear-cut at Big River Place. I missed a long shot as the bird angled away high. Eight days before Halloween, we got away from work early on a Friday and reached Arroyo Place for the last hour and a half of the hunting day to discover birds scattered around, maybe even evidence of a decent flight migrated in, as we kept stumbling on them. Afterward, we clearly recalled nine flushes, but there may have been a couple more. I never fired the gun. That may have been a record for the most flushes in a day for me without having anything close to a shot. We were back two days later, and it was snowing. An inch covered the ground, and more was falling in the form of big wet flakes that limited vision. This day produced only five flushes, but the birds were sitting much tighter, the first two coming off the ground together in the short space that separated Kristin from me. One angled low to the ground in front of me, unwilling to get more than a few feet from the blanketed forest floor. It tumbled no more than fifteen yards out when the gun barked. As I picked it up, snow fell from its feathers, the only woodcock I'd ever shot in the snow, making a special moment all the more magical. Gun unloaded, I walked with Kristin for the next few flushes as she continued to dial into flushing birds. Exactly two weeks later, on November 8, we walked the arroyo again; it now so hot it was hard to wear shirts heavy enough to protect us from the brush. No woodcock flushed.

After failing to flush any woodcock, we walked the property over. Across the trout stream, at the very back edge of the public land, a flock of turkeys melted into the woods as we approached, not allowing us to get closer than 150 yards. Heading toward these birds took us past what we refer to as a seep, a narrow stretch of land that stays perpetually wet from a spring, like a feeder stream into the bigger trout stream, but a feeder stream without an actual channel, water moving under the surface and spreading over the surface without any real confinement. Tall trees run the distance of the seep, hill to creek, with a dense understory of berry vines, buckthorn, and assorted other bushes. Farm fields lie on either side, usually planted in corn, but occasionally soybeans. This year the DNR had left eight rows of standing corn along the west side of the seep.

Everything about the seep screamed woodcock. The spots where it opened up whispered, "Hey, maybe even a snipe." But I've never seen a woodcock, let alone a snipe, there. Twice, I've found whitewash but never flushed a bird, despite it looking at least as good as the arroyo, the arroyo that has birds every year. Mysteries like this drive me, trying to figure out why cover A has birds and cover B does not. Our fishing abounds with these as well, places where two creek channels meet in a lake, with good grass cover but no bass or days that say the fish really, really, really should be doing X, but instead they are doing something as different from X as a barnyard chicken is from a snipe. Even pass shooting ducks takes a lot of figuring things out given the wind and the ground cover. If I'm set up ten yards wrong this way or that, what could have been a great morning is a nothing day instead. The question (obviously moot) is whether I would continue to do any of this if I ever got it all figured out. I mean solving the puzzle and learning new things about animal behavior is a critical aspect of my outdoor experience, but it's not all of it.

On this day, as we approached where the turkeys had vanished, a nice flock of doves came out of the standing corn and flew into the woods spanning the seep. I snapped a shot, the bird disappearing from my sight as I did. Twenty minutes of searching produced nary a feather, but it was a clue. We found doves there throughout November, flocks eating corn and roosting nearby. At times we put at least a hundred, probably two hundred, birds in the air in a single flush or as three or four groups flushed serially, nothing like what I had ever seen with doves and a great example of unexpected novelty popping up from nowhere.

In 1952 Edward Purcell won the Nobel Prize for his work in nuclear magnetic resonance, which forms the basis of the MRIs with which people are often familiar. At the heart of this work lies the notion that protons (hydrogen atom nuclei) have a magnetic axis, just as Earth has a rotational axis. That magnetic axis can wobble around an external magnetic field, another form of precession. Near the beginning of Purcell's Nobel lecture, he said, "I remember, in the winter of our first experiments, just seven years ago, looking on snow with new eyes. There the snow lay around my doorstep—great heaps of protons quietly precessing in Earth's magnetic field. To see the world for a moment as something rich and strange is the private reward of many a discovery." I am reminded of those words whenever I reflect on the novelty that arises around me, as when hundreds of doves showed up to our seep.

The massive congregation of doves stuck around until the season ended. Sometimes we got close enough for a shot. Other times we did not. Sometimes they kept circling about the area for a bit. Other times they did not. We had doves for both Thanksgiving and Christmas, making a recipe with puff pastries from the same *Game Bird Cookery* book that provided the rumaki recipe we make regularly. We've since made the puff pastry recipe with woodcock, and it may be our favorite game bird recipe, worthy of woodcock and special occasions. Imagine a holiday meal with a starter round of snipe and rail rumaki and brie en croute, followed by a main course built around puff pastry shells filled with woodcock or dove cooked with mushrooms, carrots, garlic, wine, and milk, and trout fillets encrusted with mustard and pecans. Frozen garden green beans and whatever winter squash we have on hand add to the feast that makes a gelatinous, rubbery turkey from the supermarket hard to even think about.

YEAR 22
The Flow

As we have come to expect, this year was like and unlike each of the other years in this sequence. Kristin and I started the year by teaching a course together in our January term as we had done once before. It was meant to help students consider ethical decision-making as they apply a multidisciplinary approach to an issue. Our course was titled "Recreational Use of the Natural World." We had been discussing how something like that might be fun to teach, but our schedules meant we likely would never make it work. As we'd anticipated, it was a lot of fun, particularly hearing about the students' varied experiences with the natural world. The students were, on the whole, surprised to learn about "habitat organizations" like Pheasants Forever or Ducks Unlimited, populated largely by hunters. At first, some even referred to this relationship as a "conflict of interest." The idea that one could love something like a woodcock and still want to be part of the cycle of killing and eating them is foreign to many people, as is the idea that one could pour money and time and love into the Ruffed Grouse Society and American Woodcock Society to help these birds thrive for some reason other than having more of them to shoot. These days, it seems we've reached a point where it is nearly impossible to see interactions as more than transactional. I hope we were able to do a little bit of what we always try to do—help students recognize complexity where they had seen little, help them understand different ways of looking at an issue, and help them develop tools to grapple with complex, multifaceted realities without getting lost in that complexity or resorting to unnecessary hard dichotomies, this or that and nothing in between.

I have been a longtime member of many of these organizations that so surprised the students. Ducks Unlimited was the first that I joined and has been the one I have supported the most financially over the years, for no particular reason, although the mission of building love for a seasonal wetland or mucky mosquito-breeding marsh that looks ragged and anything but tidy can be a tough one to sell. Those places do a lot of good for the world: providing carbon sequestration, habitat for all sorts of wildlife, flood mitigation, and clean water. One early February, I was in Boise, Idaho, for a work-related trip, staying at a hotel on the river, with beautiful walking trails winding by the water. It's easy to imagine that I would have built an interesting but quite different outdoor life had circumstances led me there instead of Iowa. The ducks flying along the river in the middle of the city in winter and mountains looming so near were inviting. Walking back from dinner in the hotel on the one night of my life I have spent in Idaho, I went right past a Ducks Unlimited banquet in full swing. Had I realized this event was happening I would have had dinner there instead of the hotel restaurant. After all, my luggage on that trip was a Ducks Unlimited duffel bag. As it happened though, things worked out to be interesting. During dinner, a delightful trout with lemon caper sauce, a couple at the table next to me approached and said, "We're looking forward to your show tonight." Now, I have done many planetarium shows in my life, but never are attendees quite so enthusiastic in advance. These folks had mistaken me for Livingston Taylor, who was playing a show in the same very busy hotel that night.

In the autumn fields, it was the first time in twelve years I didn't bag more than a single wood duck. We did our usual posting up for pass shooting at New Grandpa Place, but the birds—all of them—came off and were gone before legal shooting time. They didn't come back for decoying. We didn't do as much mucking around the marsh after first light as we have in the past, needing to save our legs in a way I didn't fifteen years earlier. I did, however, shoot snipe for the first time in six years, bagging two at New Grandpa Place. One October day, we flushed five or six different snipe, missing one as it startled me on the flush. It reflushed across a small ditch, and it looked as if my shot nipped it, the bird landing short in an expanse of tall marsh grass. My approach caused it to flutter a few feet and settle back before I could react. When it made another awkward flush attempt, I was ready and had my first snipe in hand in a long time. As we were exiting the marsh, Kristin worked the cattail edges while I stayed away, bordering a willow copse. She flushed a snipe that flew fifteen yards to the next cattail clump. When she flushed it again, the bird wheeled straight over me, headed for the creek beyond the willows. My first barrel was ineffective, but my second snipe of the day angled in sharply with the second report. This bird too tried to fly as I approached, but I was able to corral it, wondering at a pair of less than ideal shots in one day.

My lone duck had also failed to be a clean kill, although it landed close enough to make the retrieve straightforward. These things start to get into my head, causing me to press, trying to dial in and shoot better, but concentrating too much on shooting better isn't the thing that's going to help me shoot better. This should have been the year when I was fully back, my testosterone and muscle tone having recovered from treatment as much as they ever would, fighting against the inevitable decline. Picture the recovery as an upward arcing curve and age-related decline as a downward arcing curve, with me caught between them, trying to climb the one, forever sliding down the other. Somehow, more clean misses of birds would have felt better than all these imperfect hits, traceable all the way back to the first bird of the season, when a flock of doves got up where sunflowers met a right-angle turn of the woods at Arroyo Place. I was quick for the first attempt of the year and felt right on a bird. Feathers flew at the shot, but the bird continued, looking healthy as could be.

This shooting and hitting, wounding but (usually) retrieving continued in the woodcock woods, where the flushes were plentiful, perhaps because the birds were numerous or perhaps because we spent more time than usual focused on woodcock. Kristin had become a duck hunter, but we wanted to ensure that she was an upland hunter as well, meaning she needed to see upland birds flush. Alas, she was likely on that same age-related downward arc as I, without having had the benefit of decades of seeing birds and shouldering the gun to rely on as a sort of what people call muscle memory, the routine so ingrained that it can power you through the struggles. Working with clay pigeons helps but can only go so far. Flushing a few birds per year might work for me, less so for her as she'd begin to get dialed in and the season was gone, not to return until after long months of fishing.

Our woodcock hunting began Halloween weekend, when opening day of the pheasant season found us walking the vast open spaces up high at New Grandpa Place, an area of so-so pheasant cover. Whatever it may lack in quality, it makes up for in quantity, hard on the legs, but with a pheasant likely lurking in there somewhere. The same can be said for the clear-cuts that border the edges, narrow strips that failed to grow in as densely as you'd like, marginal but not terrible woodcock cover. Given enough time and energy expenditure, a woodcock might turn up. The lair of the Wily Woodcock was the exception to this cover of borderline quality, of course. On this day, we came up a back way on the opposite end of the property from the wetland, and we had hunted a long fruitless time when we got to the Wily Woodcock area. I wasn't sure what to feel when I saw that it had been recut, nothing there but slash. It wasn't a bad management decision given that the previous cut was well past its prime when I was last there a few years earlier, maybe a little more than a few years earlier. Understanding it was a good management decision couldn't keep me from missing what had been, knowing whatever was to be might be great but not the same as it was. No matter what I think or feel about it, life is aggressive in its drive to push forward. By the time we encountered the place now, new growth was sprouting all over, pushing up through the slash, looking as if this would once again become home to the wiliest woodcock in northeast Iowa. The question was whether I would have the legs to visit them all the way up here when the cover reached that magic age, and if I did have the legs, would I have gotten out of the habit of climbing this hill, finding woodcock elsewhere, and have forgotten all about this place of magic? We were already some distance down that road.

Our woodcock hunting gathered steam the next day, Halloween day itself. Another dreary Sunday morning rolled by at the New Grandpa Place wetland, the ducks hitting the road ten minutes before legal shooting time. Our mood changed when a woodcock spiraled down from on high, leveled out, and flew a few feet over us, squarely between us, landing in the willows beyond the ditch we had crossed on the way in. Our focus was not on finishing that duck hunt while we waited the half hour between legal duck hunting and legal woodcock hunting. The particular group of willows where this woodcock landed was one we hadn't hunted much. Three birds boiled out of it as we passed through, all in front of Kristin while I was caught in a tangle, getting pulled ever farther from her while seeking a navigable route, not hearing the birds fly. We finished the hunt in a different willow copse, one we hunted regularly, where a single woodcock flushed, maybe one that had come from the other trees, maybe not. Four flushes, no shots.

With evidence of woodcock having arrived in the local area and with our having studied the numbers sufficiently to know that this was, on average, the most productive weekend of the year, we were back out at Arroyo Place after lunch. Sometimes when we are doing year-end summaries in our journals, we are stunned by the number of days we were able to fish or hunt. But here is a key to that: not only can we walk five minutes to fish the river in town, we have many properties to both fish and hunt within a twenty-minute drive, leading to a lot of one-hour excursions. We pushed the arroyo, I with the arroyo just to my right, Kristin with the prairie grass to her left, fifteen yards separating us. Three birds came out from a single bush and headed back toward the parking lot, without offering a shot. As we continued, a woodcock appeared abruptly from behind a screen of cover, flying low and hard from left to right, having flushed between Kristin and me without my hearing it come off the ground. The bird simply materializing in front of me, gave me no time to think or worry or anything, forcing a pure instinct, quick-reaction shot. I threw my gun to my shoulder and was surprised when the little rocket angled in at the shot. I want to be clear here. This was as tough a shot as I'd had all year. To hit that bird at all was not evidence of poor shooting, but still the bird was barely clipped, another wounded bird trying to escape. There's only so much of this clean-up a soul can take. This one was particular trouble because the bird hopped down into a twisted gnarl of roots in the arroyo, where I could lose it easily, breaking my leg while giving chase. Backing off a few steps and shooting again when the bird popped briefly into the clear was certainly justified. In these instances, I aim a little high to keep from destroying the bird, this time clipping the top of the woodcock's head off, leaving only the lower half of the beak, but the breast meat fully intact. Still, I couldn't hold the bird and connect with it as usual, no eyes to lock on or head feathers to stroke down, a little gruesome and unsettling, apt for Halloween. We got two more flushes as we worked back toward the truck. We had seen at least four different birds, maybe five or six. That's a good day in the woodcock woods for us, especially following a morning of three or four elsewhere.

Our next time out, we did a split hunt at Arroyo Place and Trout-palooza Place, getting another six flushes at Arroyo Place, maybe three or four different birds. Unfortunately, they were all near me and I wasn't shooting, having already taken my bird from here. Despite producing no birds on this day, the clear-cut at Troutpalooza Place still looked good, although already showing its age, so quickly they are gone.

Exactly one week after Halloween, we did a first for us, making a trip to the lowland willows at New Grandpa Place just to hunt woodcock, no ducks or snipe, enjoying the freedom of walking these woodcock woods without the encumbrance of waders. I had not fully decided whether I was done or still hunting woodcock. We flushed one quickly without either of us seeing it. As we worked dense cover with a flooded ditch on my right, plentiful whitewash showed up between us. I was studying it as a woodcock flushed to my left, briefly clearing cover in front of me, headed toward the ditch, another fairly challenging shot that I made, deciding the question of whether I was shooting on this day, but again, the bird was merely wounded as it fell in the water. I went in over the top of my rubber boots, and the bird made it to dry land and out of view as I wallowed. I was just beginning to slip into the funk of fear that we'd lost this one, when Kristin found it. I was able to circle around to pin the bird between us for the capture. Typically, I feel greedy when I take a second woodcock in a year, and maybe I did here a bit, but having a whole bird in the hand to admire was a better way to end my season than with the Halloween bird. Continuing, we discovered that the area opened up into more willows than we had imagined existed in this spot, leading us to four more woodcock flushes. Kristin got a shot at one, the bird disappearing from sight as she fired. We kicked the cover for half an hour in hopes of locating her first woodcock, but to no avail, the bird likely having flown on unscathed.

Later in the week, we squeezed in another quick trip to Arroyo Place. Forty-five minutes of hunting produced three flushes, signaling that a few woodcock were still around. Kristin got another shot but no bird. Still, she is well on her way to being more than a duck hunter. As always, it's too bad we needed to wait another nine months to get back at it, although we both felt the inexorable flow of time, ready to turn our attention to fishing for a while. It is, as everything is, a work in progress.

My hunting season was a mess, everything slightly askew, almost but not quite right. The season included a dove I shot on the ground, flutter-hopping away, having been left there wounded by another hunter, and amid all my marginal shooting, a rail too centered in the pattern, leaving nothing but feathers and a wing. It was a decade's worth of less than ideal outcomes condensed into a single season, the pain-joy mix tilting toward pain. The bottom line result of the year was a typical number of bagged birds with a reasonable distribution of species from the usual mix of properties, a normal year when seen in a 35,000-foot flyover. Some years, however, when you drop in for a closer look, what you get is more Edvard Munch's *The Scream* than Norman Rockwell's *Freedom from Want*, the raw edge closer to the surface. All I know how to do is keep going, certain that, one way or another—or more likely one way *and* another—the next year will be different.

One of the great things about teaching anything is the often subtle fresh perspective it offers me on a topic. If I am teaching, say, Faraday's law to first-year students, it's pretty unlikely that they will have some new insight for me regarding the math of the problem. I am just too many years ahead of them in thinking about the topic, and it is one of the more challenging topics we cover—the idea that if the total amount of magnetic field over some region is changing, an electric field is created by that change. If the region is an electric circuit, then a current gets induced in that circuit. I am not convinced that any physical law has proven more important than Faraday's law for the way our technological society has evolved, including how electricity gets generated and made useful for us once it arrives at our homes. In addition to its broad application in technology, Faraday's law proved critical in helping us understand how the universe works and what light actually is. It's a theoretical as well as practical powerhouse, and every time I teach it, I find myself thinking about approaching it in a slightly new way or I stumble across an application I hadn't thought of before, keeping the topic fresh for me decades after I first tried to teach it as a graduate student in that course that started it all, when I stood at the board and that cartoon lightbulb appeared over my head.

It is possible, however, for teaching to either alter or reveal my thought on a topic in a deep and fundamental way. One of the many reasons I could likely never be a politician is that I can't imagine being in a field that punishes one for changing one's mind when encountering new facts, thinking more deeply and engaging in discourse. In the course Kristin and I were teaching this year, we asked the students to begin to make value judgments regarding spaces they deemed "natural" that they used for recreation, including ways a space may have value for many things other than recreation, forcing us to think about balancing all these different values when making decisions. For the initial stages of this work, we had the students discussing the ideas in groups of three. As they did so, Kristin and I used the opportunity to talk about why all the places we have visited in this story and hunting on those places has held so much value for us. In this discussion it was as if another cartoon lightbulb appeared above my head, and it begins to make me worry that I am slow, needing an epiphany in a classroom, for something that I should have pieced together earlier.

Suddenly, I realized that all this time in the field was a critical way for me to touch the transcendent, to feel a connection to something grander, and that astronomy served that need for me as well. They each turned out to provide macrocontact in addition to microcontact. Why it had been so critical to find a teaching instead of a research-only job was the importance of connection to those around me that came from sharing the universe's stories. For too long I had envisioned myself as a lone hunter, put off by the backslapping, needling, and competition that felt out of place in the field. Only after Kristin started hunting with me, long after my father had stopped, did I recognize how important it was to meld the microcontact with the macrocontact and how much had been missing from my time in the field, how much touching the transcendent relied on close contact with those around me.

Recognizing all this micro- and macrocontact, it's hard to envision myself as anything but blessed, the luckiest person on the face of Earth, to echo Lou Gehrig. I've often been caught telling people that it feels like a scam, making a living talking about the universe and studying the universe with bright, eager students day after day for decades. Less frequently do I have the chance to fold in how fortunate I am to have done my life's work in a place that allowed me to reconnect with the natural world, and in so doing, reconnect with the people, places, and processes from my past. When we dig potatoes every fall, I am directly connected to those long-ago years when the entire extended family gathered to dig potatoes, relying on the tubers for the sustenance not simply of starch but countless Sunday dinners that brought us together throughout the year. And while I am not sole owner of the land, places like New Grandpa Place, Old Homestead Place, Troutpalooza Place, and Arroyo Place surely are mine, places that have become home as certainly as the house where I sleep or the lab where I work with students.

Leaving aside the many other courses I have taught, the number of students I've worked with shakes out to about sixty to seventy in the research lab and between six hundred and eight hundred in the general astronomy course. These numbers seem small to me, and they are when you consider that the very first day I lectured in a physics class as a graduate student, more than six hundred undergraduates filled the enormous lecture hall. Mostly, the numbers seem small as a result of the outsized impact my interactions with these students have had on my life. I imagine them as a river flowing past, forever changed by the interaction with me and their college experience more broadly, forever changing me and the college around them, a flow expansive in both time and space, connected to the students who have come before and will come after. But this channel is also linked to a greater network of channels, like a web encompassing the globe.

I can see this web in flowing waters that have helped make my life what it is. Having had the good fortune to be raised in a time and place where it was deemed acceptable—good, in fact—to see off a child for an entire morning or afternoon of wading a creek that ran half a mile away, I was in the water fishing and exploring every summer day. The days were filled with catching bluegill, bullhead, chubs, and shiners and hooking the occasional behemoth of a carp that would thrash the surface to a froth when it felt the tiny hook. A couple of years before this last in our story, Kristin and I were back visiting and went to fish that childhood creek. Below a low-head dam that creates a reflecting pool beneath a bank that sits in the vee of two bridges where highways meet, we each hooked thick smallmouth bass. Kristin landed hers, mine breaking the four-pound test line in the fast water. These bronze monsters were fish that never populated the dreams of a small child catching chubs and sunfish, but from that dam it is a short run of unobstructed water to a river that is formed in a park in town where two other rivers meet, and these other rivers were major producers of smallmouth for me when I was old enough to spread my wings and get more adventurous with my exploration.

Generally, the rivers that meet in the park are good for floating using a tube or canoe, moving neither too quickly nor too slowly for a day of fishing, but they get sluggish near their confluence. It was that sluggishness, I suppose, as well as the folly of youth, that led my friend and me to decide to carry along a trolling motor and battery in our canoe on one trip. It was our first such outing after the months of struggle that culminated in my tonsillectomy and the irritable bowel that has tracked me since. As such, we thought that while the fresh air and fishing would surely provide healing sustenance, the motor would save undue wear and tear on me. Of course, we could have opted for something shorter than an all-day adventure under the hot Sun, but that never crossed our minds. The extra weight in the already heavy metal canoe made the early going tough as we dragged bottom in spots that we hadn't expected. The canoe needed pulling free on several occasions before we rounded a corner to find our biggest obstacle of the day, the most impressive logjam I've ever encountered on any river at any time in my life, never before or after having seen anything close. Logs, full-grown sycamore trees, were jammed in at all angles, wedged shore to shore, towering over us to a height three times our own and extending two hundred yards or more downriver. If one reason for this excursion had been to turn my mind from the year that had been, then it was at least a partial success. The portage of canoe, motor, battery, and enough tackle to win a bass tournament through dense cover and along sheer, crumbling mud walls made the months of health woes I had just endured seem like a barefoot walk on a sand beach bathed in the glow of soft evening light.

The creek that flowed through the land where my father was raised had a different feel from the in-town creek, in part exotic because I was unable to spend every day exploring it but also because it was sur-rounded by wilder land. This creek had large gray slabs of what surely was some sort of mudstone with soft marl exposed by the flowing water, but which we kids called "soapstone" because we could tear off chunks, using them to write on other stones scattered around. Most summers this creek dried to the point that the flow stopped, leaving sunfish piled into disconnected deeper pools. I tried catching these fish some, but even as a young child I recognized the painful, unsporting nature of this "fish in a barrel" angling. I'd give up after the first few vicious strikes the instant my lure hit the water, instead spending an hour capturing grasshoppers in the dry grasses bordering the creek and feeding them to those trapped fish, hoping at least a few could hang on until the stream flowed once more.

The water from that country creek flowed into the larger Hoosier National Forest creek where my mom dropped me on that tick-filled day years ago; there it flows past a spot on the USGS topographical map called Wilkerson Hill. I asked my father about it once, and he replied, "Must be some other Wilkersons." Really, what are the odds of that? Not terribly long before I was born, this stream was dammed to create Indiana's largest reservoir, and I've spent many days working its upper reaches, where it is impossible to discern lake from inflow creek. Of course, the creek reemerges from the dam, and once it does, it flows a short distance before disappearing into the same river that was formed by the confluence of rivers in the park in my hometown. That river flows into Indiana's most famous river of song and story, the Wabash, which in turn disappears into the Ohio not far from where the Tennessee merges with the Ohio, the Tennessee being the river dammed to make the The Lake, a web of connections strung together by life-giving water. Not far after where the Tennessee joins the Ohio, the Ohio and Mississippi merge, the Mississippi having carried down water from my current home, trout streams so important in the story of my most recent quarter century having emptied into the river flowing by my house and on into the big river.

When I teach the general astronomy course, the most important linchpins are the stories of the move from geocentrism to heliocentrism and our understanding of spiral nebulae as external galaxies rather than gas clouds within our Milky Way. These are, perhaps obviously, critical because they are stories of our developing understanding of our place in the universe as well as the scale of the universe. For our course, these are also important stories for the people at their heart, how they went about their work, and how they interacted with one another, every one of us reminded that astronomy, all science, is a human endeavor undertaken by real human beings with beating hearts and flowing blood. Just as important, we see the differences between those two studies and yet the similarities that connect them. We can start to see the human study of the universe as a single story flowing through space and time so that the flow connects the characters of the heliocentrism story—Tycho Brahe, Johannes Kepler, Galileo Galilei, etc.—with the characters of the spiral nebula story—Heber Curtis, Harlow Shapley, Vesto Slipher, Adriaan van Maanen, Edwin Hubble, etc.—with the characters of more recent stories—Jocelyn Bell, Chushiro Hayashi, George Smoot, Vera Rubin, Saul Perlmutter, etc. Surely, with our work together in a course or in the research lab, we can see ourselves as a part of that flow. When I take data, shooting my repetitive images, after things are set up, when equipment is ready to run for the night but it's not yet sufficiently dark to start, I sit on the stairs to the observing deck and watch the stars emerging from the darkening sky. At that moment I not only feel tied to the flow of human effort to understand the universe but to all the parts of the universe.

When I walk the woods and marshes, I feel not only connected to my family but to the characters of *Anna Karenina* and to all the hunters who have walked this land before me, who have roamed anywhere on the face of Earth, extracting a living from that Earth, and joined with all those who will come after me and do the same. My story is mine alone but shared with all these others.

I recall reading a story long ago in which the author claimed to have a unique perspective on Mario Lemieux's return to hockey after cancer treatment, the author's having had the same type of cancer as Lemieux. I thought at the time (and still think) that nothing could be further from the truth, each person's experience with any illness, even the common cold, being thoroughly unique to that person. My cancer journey is like no one else's, and yet nothing could connect us more. During my years of treatment, each floor of the clinic had its own vibe—the madding bustle of Urology, the quiet serenity of Medical Oncology, the steady down to business churn—somewhere between the other two—of Radiation Oncology. Each stop was filled with faces at different places in the battle, each fighting a different battle but all of us connected in some way, just as we were linked through space to people all over the world engaged in similar struggles, seen and unseen, and attached through time to people who had come before us and who are still to come, waking today or tomorrow or in the next millennium to a forever-altered reality when they learn they have their version of that disease that we were all fighting together and all fighting alone.

Near the beginning of this meandering narrative, I speculated that I had measured out my life one woodcock at a time and wondered about the worth of such a measure. That is but one measure, however. Just as surely, I have measured out my life in the return to the sky of Sagittarius each spring and in the flights of wood ducks each spring and fall. I have measured out my life in digging potatoes each fall and in the arrival of each new class of students ready to begin their journeys in earnest. I have measured out my life in float tube adventures and in each new morning when I see my wife's eyes for another day. All the threads connecting all the moments are vibrating, creating music.

ACKNOWLEDGMENTS

I owe the greatest debt to my parents who, among all the things they did for me, understood I was better off outdoors and demonstrated that it was possible to grow every vegetable one would eat and to fill a freezer with fish. I wish that over the years I had been able to repay a tiny fraction of that debt. I am grateful for all my Luther College colleagues and students. I have learned something from each of them. I am particularly grateful to those who were instrumental in hiring me: Dick Kellogg, Dennis Barnaal, Randy Brown, and Bob Larson. To this day I don't know what they saw in me. A special thanks goes to all who worked meticulously on the text at the University of Iowa Press, particularly Meredith Stabel and Carolyn Brown. The text is far more readable thanks to their efforts. The joy I find in all things has been amplified immensely by sharing adventures every day with my wife, Kristin. My delight in the natural world, the mysteries of the universe, and teaching surely would have faded without her.